reflections ON PRACTICE

Series editor: Mike Calvert

Reflections on ICT

Edited by Terry Atkinson

CiLT
Centre for Information on Language Teaching and Research

The views expressed in this book are those of the editor and contributors and do not necessarily reflect the views of CILT.

First published 2001
by the Centre for Information on Language Teaching and Research (CILT)
20 Bedfordbury, London WC2N 4LB

ISBN 1 902031 93 8

A catalogue record for this book is available from the British Library

Printed in Great Britain by Copyprint UK Ltd

CILT Publications are available from: **Central Books,** 99 Wallis Rd, London E9 5LN. Tel: 0845 458 9910. Fax: 0845 458 9912. Book trade representation (UK and Ireland): **Broadcast Book Services,** Charter House, 27a London Road, Croydon CR0 2RE. Tel: 020 8681 8949. Fax: 020 8688 0615.

Reflections on ICT

reflections ON PRACTICE

Other titles in the series

Reflections on Citizenship in a multilingual world
Ed. Kim Brown and Margot Brown
REFLECTIONS ON PRACTICE 8

Reflections on motivation
Ed. Gary Chambers
REFLECTIONS ON PRACTICE 6

Reflections on grammar-implicit teaching
Margaret Wells
REFLECTIONS ON PRACTICE 5

Reflections on the target language
Peter S Neil
REFLECTIONS ON PRACTICE 4

Reflections on Modern Languages in primary education: six UK case studies
Ed. Alison Hurrell and Peter Satchwell
REFLECTIONS ON PRACTICE 3

Reflections on reading: from GCSE to A level
Ed. Mike Grenfell
REFLECTIONS ON PRACTICE 2

Contents

Book web page

The editor has created a web page for this book which gives up-to-date addresses for all web references. Readers might find it useful to bookmark this page for ease of linking to the sites in the book, avoiding possible re-typing errors as well as broken links. This web page is located on the CILT website at: www.cilt.org.uk/refict.htm.

Introduction – ICT in language learning: from enhancement to transformation

Terry Atkinson

Communication via the medium of Information and Communications Technology (ICT) knows few bounds. New ways of using this global medium are emerging all the time. If you want to place a prayer on the Wailing Wall but can't make it to Jerusalem, you can e-mail your prayer to the website[1] and someone will print it out and put it on the wall for you (provided you have a credit card and can afford the delivery charges!). Technology often provides solutions to problems that are not yet identified. When Alexander Graham Bell invented the telephone, he imagined that the use of his invention would extend only as far as each town having one telephone in the mayor's office. The computer, having been invented as a number crunching device, is now pivotal to communication and a central element of what we have come to know as ICT encompassing a range of tools such as audio, video and telephony.

Herein lies a challenge for all involved in the teaching and learning of modern foreign languages. How can these tools be best exploited to support learning? This is the question that the contributors to the current volume are seeking to answer. They are engaged variously in researching, evaluating and reflecting upon their experiences. This process of critical enquiry is essential since we have here not a simple question of how to exploit a given resource but rather one of how to adapt to constantly evolving and emerging technologies. As Fullan (1993) has argued, this is not simply the need to adapt to change – we have to accept change as the norm. ICT is not to be defined in terms of a set of tools but rather as a historical moment characterised by rapid technological change.

Figure 1 charts the introduction of new tools to the language learning process and their impact on it. Beginning as an enhancement of the learning process, there is a steady shift of emphasis leading to substantial change if not total transformation. Bruner (1990) suggests that computers have the capacity to '*redefine the natural limits of human functioning*' (p21) and, if this is so, it follows that such functions as teaching and learning of languages must also now be redefined. However, while technology changes at an ever increasing rate, pedagogy sometimes takes longer to keep up, leading to what Barson (1998) terms a decalage between the two. In the hurly burly of the modern school there is often little time to step back and reflect upon emerging pedagogy. Hence, we present here a collection of studies in which teachers do precisely that. Some of the studies consider relatively new technologies while others focus on tried and trusted programs. Many of the studies relate to resources that have been around for some time such as e-mail, Internet and videoconferencing. These all present excellent opportunities for language learning, but they also provide a classic illustration of Barson's decalage in that finding the appropriate ways of exploiting them is problematic.

	Tool	Impact on learning
1960s	reel to reel tape recorders	listening
1970s	language laboratories	listening / speaking
1980s	video and OHP	visual
1990s	IT	reading and writing
2000s	ICT	interaction / collaboration
2010s	virtual learning	autonomy

Figure 1: Technological innovation in language learning

The book falls into three parts. Part One has a research focus, based primarily on classrooms and learners. All of these studies come from participant observers in which reflection and evaluation are the principal methods of enquiry. In Part Two, we present a series of shorter and more anecdotal case studies by practitioners in which they describe innovative ways of using technology and reflect upon the outcomes. Running through the book is a concern with the impact of ICT on language learning. A secondary focus, more apparent in one or two of the case studies, is the way in which teachers are using new technologies and the effect on the role of the teacher. The chapter in Part Three considers the longer term implications of new technologies for tomorrow's teachers.

Technology, communication and language skills

The exploitation of ICT in the teaching and learning process has been considered for some time, but latterly there has been an explosion in computer-mediated communication which has implications for what we teach as well as the way we teach it. The use of ICT for communication has become so prevalent that it is itself a key skill for language users and an important outcome of using ICT in learning. Arguably, ICT implies a new literacy or a fifth skill in language use. So what is this fifth skill? Its essence is the ability to access information, to assess meaning and validity, to process and adapt language, to create meaning and to communicate using increasingly diverse media.

Finding information on the World Wide Web calls for a mix of technical and linguistic skills. The use of browsers, navigation aids, hyperlinks, search engines, web crawlers and web guides is part of the technical toolkit needed. Linguistically, the web places a premium on knowing superordinate words because these provide the key to being able to decide which links to follow for different categories of information. Learners need the confidence to use links to formulate and test hypotheses. Simple treasure trails give practice in both technical and linguistic skills. In Helen Wright's chapter there is an interesting discussion of the new reading skills that learners are deploying in web-based reading. There are implications here for readers at all levels. The Internet passed the one billion users mark in the year 2000, so what will become of those with reading difficulties? The Web is changing many aspects of the way we live and one of these is to increase dependency on the written word. It is vital to support learners in developing their reading skills and to realise that new reading skills are involved as part of the emerging new literacy. This may be a temporary effect since more advanced systems will enable much more voice based communication. Already, a new generation of text to voice software[2] will read e-mails, web pages, word documents and any other text. Unsurprisingly, this software is available initially in English only.

Learners need to be able to make sense of the information they find on the Web. As Grellet (1981) argues, in considering any text, it is important to begin with macro features such as design, layout, context, organisation and style. For a democratic medium like the Web, the first step has to be to assess the origin and validity of the information. A simple example might be deciding who has published the page by looking at the URL – from what country does it come and is it from a company, a government or a private individual? Atkinson (1998) has more on how to work this out from the URL and sophisticated tutorials such as the *Internet Detective*[3] offer excellent advice and guidance on establishing the status of material from the Web. By way of example, students can develop the skill of validation through comparing the approach of different sources to the same issue, e.g. compare newspapers in different countries reporting on an international incident. As Harry Fairtlough points out, evaluation is a vital skill for teachers as they make increasing use of the Web as a source of authentic materials and of teaching and learning materials.

The skill of processing, redrafting, adapting, paraphrasing, summarising and citing texts created by others is an important one which enables learners to enhance their work rather than simply copying and pasting the language and images that they find. Many teachers have experience of learners who give in as their own work printouts from CD-ROMs or the Web. Such crude plagiarism is relatively easy to detect, but is there something more fundamental to be considered here? When and how is it appropriate to recycle information? Students need the opportunity to practise and develop a range of skills that will enable the legitimate use of sources. These skills include knowing how to and when to use the following:

- computerised translation;
- quotation and referencing;
- paraphrasing and summarising;
- a range of sources;
- a synthesis of key ideas.

Again, tasks can be set which encourage the development of these skills. As a follow-on to the activity in which students compare newspapers in different countries reporting on an international incident, they might then produce a simple presentation orally or perhaps with the aid of presentation software, highlighting the key differences between the two accounts of the same incident. The pedagogy for teaching such skills is not difficult to develop, but it is important that the skill itself is targeted. New learning objectives emerge as new technologies appear and here we may see a shift away from writing towards researching and adapting.

With the invention of print, the ancients feared the end of knowledge creation since everything would be written down and there would be no need for constant reinterpretation in the way that the oral medium had demanded. This spectre again looms with the advent of the World Wide Web. Why write something if everything is there already? Just log on to homework.com and download an essay from a choice of several dozen. And yet, just as print has expanded enormously the creative process, so too can the Web and the use of a range of other ICT tools.

Drafting, redrafting and creative writing are core ICT activities. Word processing, presentation software, web page creation tools and desktop publishing all offer mechanisms for drafting and presenting ideas. Tools such as spellcheckers, thesauruses, electronic dictionaries, grammar checkers, translation software and concordancers provide support for students to check the accuracy of their own work. Future developments will increasingly mean that spoken as well as written language can be crafted with the help of the technology. We glimpse this already in the videoconferencing case studies reported by Philip Dobison and Garry Hudson and in the account of the use of telephony in distance learning by Sue Hewer and Lesley Shield. In the near future, webcasting will make it possible for schools and colleges to broadcast their own radio and television programmes.

ICT is a communications medium par excellence, allowing global publication via the Web, multimedia presentation, e-mail and videoconferencing for individuals and groups. The development of virtual worlds and on-line communities offers exciting possibilities for language learners to become language users in real interactive contexts without leaving home, as Lesley Shield et al show. Communication via e-mail is growing rapidly. Think only of the havoc caused by viruses bringing down e-mail and it is apparent that many large organisations can no longer function if their e-mail systems crash. Checking your e-mail is a routine activity for many individuals. For the moment at least, the medium is primarily text-based and asynchronous and so gives prominence to reading and writing skills – a quick scan through your inbox will reveal the fact that some of your correspondents are better at this than others and that there is a wide range of approaches. We are all learning how to communicate through this medium, developing in the process a whole new discourse and one taken several steps further by the advent of text messaging on mobile phones. However, there is also a sense in which the tool we use changes the nature of communication. For language students, reading e-mails or text messages and replying to them are key skills to be learned, and communicating via these media provides the opportunity to interact with native speakers and to develop and practise skills.

Read the videoconferencing case studies by Dobison and Hudson and you will be left in no doubt as to the authenticity of the communication process that this medium facilitates. Students engage in detailed preparation for the videoconference because it is a real live task in real time. They concentrate during the conference as if their lives depend upon it. The post conference debrief provides a wonderful opportunity for formative feedback.

Learning

The role of ICT in language learning has been consistently challenged. What is the impact on learning and what is added by the use of technology that could not be achieved by other means? These questions may be reasonable, but the very fact that they are asked is also quite telling. It reflects a degree of uncertainty over the value of technology which is based upon the relative newness of the medium, shortage of hardware and software in schools and technical difficulties in using these resources which, at times, reverse the decalage highlighted by Barson between technology and pedagogy – teachers are well aware of how they would like to make use of ICT but can't gain access to it!

In fact, it is hard to prove any substantial impact on learning. Cox (1993) identifies the problem of lack of systematic access. Since it is rare for a class to have extended and systematic access to ICT for language learning, it is difficult to detect any real impact on learning. Limited access to hardware leads to a situation in which most classes will make only occasional use of ICT. Exceptionally, a class may undertake an ICT project over the course of a month with four or five computer lessons. In these circumstances, it is very difficult to isolate any longer term impact on learning or to conclude that any improvements in motivation would be sustained as the novelty wears off. The studies in this book illustrate many of the potential benefits of using the technology and some of the disadvantages. It may be difficult to prove that ICT improves learning, but only in the same way that it is difficult to prove that books or audio tapes improve learning. Moreover, ICT does not so much improve learning as transform it. Thus, any real impact on learning will necessitate changes to curricula and assessment frameworks and not just to teaching and learning methods.

Nevertheless, the use of ICT can enhance the learning process in many different ways. Levels of motivation are seen to be raised for many learners when using ICT. This effect is reported very commonly by teachers and researchers and often in terms of genuine astonishment at the degree of commitment shown by students. This may be due to the novelty of using ICT and to the project approach that often characterises ICT work. It is difficult to say what the effect on motivation would be if the computer replaced the exercise book as a routine classroom tool. Not all learners are comfortable with computers and some find them very off-putting. Motivation also varies according to the nature of the activity being undertaken, the ease of use of the equipment, the learning environment and so on. While it is difficult to guarantee motivation through use of ICT, it is clear enough that many learners respond very well to the medium. Lesley Hagger-Vaughan's chapter conveys the strength of response of her target learners, but it is interesting to note that the learners report different reactions to different applications and can often highlight very precise reasons for this, usually connected to a perception of how specific skills have been developed.

From a humble printout on an ageing dot-matrix printer to all singing all dancing multimedia, technology enables students to produce work to much more professional standards than would otherwise be possible. This confers status on the work itself even if a closer examination reveals errors in language and content. It makes students' work accessible to a wider audience, enabling collaboration with other learners. Thus, realistic tasks can be designed in which learners work together in a creative enterprise: a class magazine, a website, a multimedia presentation or a videoconference with a link school.

Presentation is closely allied to the quality of the end product. Because the computer allows work to be edited and altered, a more sophisticated outcome can be achieved. It is possible to draft, to redraft, to develop and to extend a piece of work. A piece of writing produced in Year 7 can be worked on again a year or more later. This brings opportunities for longer term projects.

Technology provides access to an amazing diversity of authentic resources in the target language from every corner of the globe. Today's weather forecast can be found in the target language for any reasonably sized place on the planet. Moreover, the forecast may only be available in text and images at present, but this will be in full colour and the advent of broad band Internet access will mean that audio and video versions will become available. The Internet, CD-ROMs, digital television, mobile phones and other emerging technologies bring access to a vast range of up-to-the-minute resources. Developing the pedagogical skills to exploit all of this is a daunting challenge, but the opportunity is there to allow learners choice in materials, activities and contexts. It is possible to select virtually any inhabited centre in the world and access directly local information such as the newspaper, schools, shopping, local government, radio station, maps, photographs, personal web pages of local residents, industries, health and welfare services, clubs and sporting organisations, cultural and leisure pursuits, tourist information and much more.

Access to resources for lesser taught languages is greatly boosted through technology as demonstrated in Jim Anderson's chapter. Hewer and Shield note also the potential use of VLEs (Virtual Learning Environments) for the teaching of languages where *class numbers do not justify the provision of a face-to-face teacher*.

Through the use of tools such as e-mail, videoconferencing and the Web, it is now possible to meet and communicate with people from around the world. Virtual exchanges with students who are native speakers open up interesting new possibilities for learning, collaboration and communication as shown in several of the contributions to this book. These activities may be the prelude to an actual exchange or visit but are also worthwhile in their own right since communication via technology is as much a part of the real world as face-to-face communication. For many years now the first contact with native speakers has been via technology – audio and video tape. It is now possible to talk back! Again, the pedagogical exploitation of the technology is at an experimental stage.

When learners use tools they are more active in their learning. This learning by doing is ultimately more meaningful and, therefore, more memorable than learning by watching or learning by being told. Open ended tasks can allow learners to create their own meanings and carefully structured tasks can provide the opportunity for students to learn through experimentation, by making mistakes and through the non-judgemental feedback provided by the computer. Not all students are comfortable with active learning styles. Some may prefer more time to reflect whereas working on a computer tends to impose an imperative to do something – there isn't much time for sitting and thinking during a videoconference with a partner school in Spain. Nevertheless, for many learners, active learning is a rewarding experience.

Instant correction of computer-based exercises which is non-judgemental and private is one of the features that computers can provide and that is not readily available by other means. This works best for situations in which there is one answer, such as a multiple choice test or a text reconstruction activity. The addition of sound, pictures and video to such activities is a considerable enhancement, but even the more basic early offerings have shown that they engage learners in thinking about and discussing language in ways which are not often seen in the languages classroom. Heather Rendall's chapter points to the fact that students can develop a better grasp of the application of grammar to language through systematic practice with interactive software. Unsurprisingly perhaps, it turns out that carefully structured exercises with instant feedback consolidate learning. What is surprising is the way in which the learners retain and recover their skills. The interactive feedback loop has tremendous potential to enable learners to induce and infer patterns intuitively.

Since different learners achieve differing results with different resources, it is probable that there will be parallels in the use of ICT resources. Some learners will do better than others. Some will relish using a medium with which they are familiar and in which they are skilled, while others may react against it whether for psychological reasons, e.g. computer phobia or learned helplessness, physical reasons (the flickering monitor and whirring drives do upset some people), or a preference for different learning styles; more reflection or social interaction perhaps. For some learners, the technology presents a new range of learning difficulties such as the heavy concentration on reading, often with small print in unfamiliar fonts and difficult colour combinations. Or the need to cope with keyboard and mouse which dyspraxic or uncoordinated children find difficult unless given access to alternative hardware and software options that cater for learners with such difficulties, e.g. pointing and input devices. Using technology to overcome learning difficulties is standard practice. Technology can support learners and some studies (Clements et al 1998) show that the impact of technology on learning is most apparent with lower achievers. On that admittedly small scale study, it appeared that higher achievers are confident in a range of learning contexts and usually do well whatever the approach. For some lower achievers, the use of technology enabled them to reach a higher level than they otherwise would. Support for a specific, identified learning difficulty is seen in David Wilson's study of foreign handwriting difficulties and the use of special fonts to provide extended practice opportunities. Here is one of the key strengths of ICT – it makes it possible to design and deliver specialised, differentiated or individualised learning activities.

For the language learner, a new set of skills and strategies must be developed. As well as knowing how to move the mouse pointer and operate the button to click on an icon, one also has to decide when and what to click on so as to form and test hypotheses rather than to lose oneself in cyberspace or baffle oneself with endless streams of information. As Helen Wright argues, the Web is not simply a medium in which one rehearses the traditional reading skills of skimming and scanning, but rather one in which there is a whole new literacy to be acquired. The visual syntax of a web page is clearly different to that of a newspaper or a book because of the increased interactivity of the medium. Similarly, using interactive CALL software is comparable to, but different from, doing paper and pen exercises from the board or a text book. Heather Rendall's study shows how learners can acquire patterns through using technology that frees their minds to make intuitive judgements. Here, the technology provides rapid feedback which, Rendall argues, is indispensable for the learning to take hold. However, the rapid feedback comes about only if the learners have the skills to quickly input their answers and the confidence to have a go and learn as much from errors as from getting it right.

New learning strategies are needed for learners to communicate through the new technologies. In Jim Anderson's study, the students undertake research into content, look at examples as models for their own creative work, consider the audience they are writing for, design the layout of their work for the specific medium of the Web and draft and redraft the content in a range of media. Thorough preparatory work is vital to the success of videoconferences, with similar but different skills being deployed in this more orally based medium. Both web publishing and videoconferencing place a premium on effective preparation since the end product is real communication with native speakers.

Teaching

Technology is steadily changing the nature of the role of teachers and the tasks that they routinely carry out. Consider this list of tasks that teachers might now be required to do as part and parcel of daily school routine:

- use electronic devices for calling the register;
- use the Internet to research a topic;
- send an e-mail request to a discussion forum;
- prepare exercises on computer for a lesson in the IT room;
- use an interactive whiteboard or TV connected to a PC for part of a lesson;
- prepare worksheets using word processing software;
- use videoconferencing equipment or e-mail for a virtual exchange;
- use the Internet to access a range of official documentation such as OFSTED reports, National Curriculum details, examination syllabuses;
- complete computer based records on pupils' progress;
- use a spreadsheet to store and analyse pupils' assessment results;
- contribute to the development of a school/departmental website.

Few of these tasks were even dreamed of ten years ago and yet it is now apparent that this trend will continue with more and more technologically based tasks becoming part of the language teacher's routine. Some tasks are simply a matter of using a slightly different tool for a broadly similar purpose, but others imply a changing role for teachers, moving them further along the path towards managers/facilitators of learning rather than imparters of knowledge. Hewer and Shield argue that technological innovations can only be harnessed by those teachers who *'can adapt to the changed role of facilitator and manager of learning, rather than knowledge source'*. Lesley Hagger-Vaughan describes a lesson in which the students *'hung up their coats and just got on with one of the allocated tasks – one or two had a chat in the cloakroom and I held back from telling them to get on with it. Five minutes later the whole of the class were on task – completely independently'*.

The selection of studies in this book is almost wholly concerned with student-centred learning and this is not merely a result of editorial bias. It seems that the impact of technology is decisively oriented towards greater student independence and autonomy. This in itself makes possible the action research stance adopted by the teachers in the studies that follow. The move from delivery of teaching to management of learning brings with it new opportunities for the evaluation of the effectiveness of the learning. Moreover, an action research approach is needed to ensure that the innovative tools and methods are beneficial. As the pace of innovation quickens, the need to monitor is greater.

Assessment is crucial in this technological age and that area is also transformed by technology. Computer based assessment via CALL packages and integrated learning systems yield masses of data. The focus of assessment moves from product to process as students use increasingly sophisticated tools in completing tasks – web searching, CD-ROMs, spell checking, thesaures, concordancers and translation software. Teachers are using technology to support assessment, for example the use of on-screen revisions to mark word processed work, e-mail to supply feedback, spreadsheets to compile and analyse marks, databases to track progress and integrated packages to generate reports. The greatest challenge in the area of assessment is the need to bring into the assessment framework the new language skills ushered in by changing technology and changing communications media. *Reply to the following e-mail* is not yet a routine examination task, in part because it would require students to use computers during the examination.

Teachers now have tools which can enhance and extend their professional role. The technology empowers them to create and publish. Moreover, it networks practitioners and facilitates collaboration. The Virtual Teachers Centre was set up with this potential in mind. However, there is no limit to what a few like-minded individual teachers can do as they work together in what amounts to a virtual working party. This book is a humble example of what can be achieved via technology since most of the contributors were found via the Linguanet discussion forum. A single e-mail to the forum produced dozens of offers of contributions. Naturally, e-mail was then used to negotiate these and to exchange abstracts, drafts and comments. Taking this one stage further, it is questionable how much longer CILT will publish books such as this when they can be readily published on the Internet. The same approach can be applied to a host of other projects. Consider these:

course materials – working with a group of colleagues and publishing your own language course on the Web;

schemes of work – the DfEE are lending a hand with their website[4];

interactive exercises for language students;

students' work on the Web;

web-based professional portfolios for teachers;

articles for on-line journals;

chapters for on-line books;

virtual learning environments;

virtual student exchanges and school links via e-mail, Web and videoconferencing;

teachers' discussion fora;

networks of action researchers on the Internet;

virtual tutoring by Internet telephony and videoconferencing;

classroom observation through videoconferencing for initial training or further professional development;

classroom based research via videoconferencing or webcam;

partnership in initial teacher training at a distance via telecommunications;

web-based research to enhance subject knowledge of students and teachers;

dissemination of professional information via the Internet– syllabuses, OFSTED reports, learning materials, teaching techniques.

An example of the immediacy of web-based publishing is provided by Jessica Smith who has constructed a website[5] giving guidance on how to pass A level French. In fact, she did this just after sitting her A levels and her motivation for creating the site was that she had not been able to find the sort of advice that she was seeking.

Conclusion

The information age brings about a transformation in schooling which will have far reaching effects for the teaching and learning of languages. For the first time, ICT will be one of the most significant aspects in this subject area. The percentage of ICT-based language learning is likely to grow rapidly until it is indispensable. The nature of schooling will be altered as children spend less time in bricks and mortar classrooms and more in virtual ones. In some countries, government policy is already decreeing rapid change. For example, in Hong Kong, the Education and Manpower Bureau's strategy calls for 25% of the curriculum to be taught with the help of ICT by the end of the school year 2002–2003. Inevitably, change brings with it problems and there are important issues to be resolved such as:

access to hardware and software for language learners at school, at home and in the community – not just networked PCs but powerful communications networks facilitating rapid exchange of full multimedia;

development of pedagogy appropriate to the new and emerging technologies, e.g. virtual learning, on-line tutoring, videoconferencing;

ICT skills for teachers so that they can exploit the medium for a full range of professional purposes;

redefinition of professional roles as teaching, training, researching, publishing and the like become increasingly blurred;

building international and global partnerships between professionals, schools, HEIs, publishers, technology companies, etc;

funding for classroom based research on the use of new technologies and dissemination of findings.

While computers may never replace teachers, those teachers who do not learn how to integrate ICT into language learning will be replaced by those who do. The advent of the dot coms has seen the replacement of face-to-face or telephone sales of airline tickets, hotel reservations and even groceries. In the world of language learning it may be that our students will soon opt to learn their languages in virtual classrooms where they can choose where, when and what to learn. In the year 2000, the percentage of virtual language learning by secondary school students was probably in single figures, perhaps even less than one per cent. In higher education, it was already growing in significance. Undergraduates were beginning to sit examinations at a computer terminal and trainee teachers were to take tests in literacy, numeracy and in 2002 also in ICT in this mode. It is inevitable, therefore, that the percentage of time spent on virtual language learning and assessment will grow steadily in the *noughties*.

Bibliography

Atkinson T, *WWW: The Internet* (CILT, 1998)

Barson J, 'Dealing with double evolution: action-based learning approaches and instrumental technology' *World CALL Conference,* (University of Melbourne, 1998)

Bruner J, *Acts of meaning* (Harvard University Press, 1990)

Clements B, B Gath, P Standen, A Barnes and P Haezewindt, 'Project report (unpublished)', summarised in Atkinson T, *Researching language learning and technology,* World CALL Conference, (University of Melbourne, 1998)

Cox M, 'Technology enriched school project – the impact of information technology on children's learning' in *Computer Education,* Vol 21: (1993)

Fullan M, *Change forces* (Falmer, 1993)

Grellet F, *Developing reading skills: a practical guide to reading comprehension exercises* (Cambridge University Press, 1981)

Notes

1 www.wailingwall.com/
2 See for example *Readplease* at www.readplease.com/
3 www.sosig.ac.uk/desire/internet-detective.html
4 www.standards.dfee.gov.uk/schemes2/secondary_mff/>
5 www.frenchalevelhelp.hemscott.net/

PART ONE

Research studies

In this part we present four research studies, each of which considers the role of ICT in the learning of languages from both a theoretical and practical perspective. These studies draw on considerable practical experience with learners in classrooms and other learning situations. They are also grounded in the literature that has developed around the study of language learning and ICT. Where direct reference to this literature is made, the reference is supplied, although there has been no aim to provide a substantial bibliography or literature review. Two of the chapters, Rendall and Anderson, present in summary the findings from work that was designed as doctoral studies. All of the authors are minded to present their work for an audience of practitioners who may be interested in aspects of research design and in the literature but who will be more concerned with the applicability of the outcomes of the research.

These four chapters present a systematic account of the ways in which technology can transform language learning. What emerges is not a tour de force of technological wizadry - some of the studies deal with quite basic tools. Rather, it is a question of carefully analysing the usefulness of quite specific solutions: handwriting fonts, word sequencing, web publishing and Internet telephony. Each of these is shown to enhance learning in a particular context once an appropriate pedagogy has been developed or adapted from existing practice.

Chapter 1

Developing a greater sense of gender in French: ICT integration at initial learner level

Heather Rendall

This chapter deals with one aspect of a research project, designed as part of an intended doctoral thesis investigating the potential of ICT to create cognitive patterns and learning strategies. The need for new cognitive patterns is established by a comparison of language distances, in which grammar gaps are pinpointed. The physical requirements to create neurological connections and neural pathways in the brain are discussed and compared to the demands imposed by the programming of a relatively simple and unsophisticated piece of software. Isolating from the mass of material recorded over a three-year period those exercises and results which concentrated on gender, the author is able to show that a group of twelve pupils, who alone had regular access to a particular computer program, seemed to develop the ability to outperform their peers not just in highly focused tests but, by the end of Key Stage 3, in the production of free writing as well.

Corder (1978:11) coined the phrase *'language distance'* to describe two things: firstly the measurement of dissimilarity between the grammar of two languages; and secondly the difficulty that this dissimilarity imposes on the learner. If there could possibly be two languages whose grammatical structures were exactly similar, then language distance would be reduced to nil: language learning would be a matter of learning words and transliterating thoughts from the mother tongue into the target language. But no two languages are like that. English, closely related as it is to French and German, has over the years since separation and independence, either borrowed, adapted or thrown out characteristics of one or other parent, thus creating more and more distance between it and them.

And it is the latter move – the abandoning of major grammatical characteristics – that is at the core of this study. *'If the (target language) does not contain the grammatical categories the learner is used to from his (mother tongue), he will be confronted with a basic initial learning problem'* (Ringbom 1989). This study focuses on how to help students handle one such problem – gender.

English, unlike other European languages, has dispensed with the categorisation of nouns into gender. Tied inextricably to gender comes agreement, which in English has been reduced to number (singular and plural: *he* > *they* : *this* > *these*) and person (*the man* > *he* : *the woman* > *she*: but *the dog* > *it*). The English definite and indefinite articles have been worn down to an invariable *the* and *a* (though it does use *an* in front of a vowel): there is no nominal adjective agreement at all.

This lack of two of the grammatical features which characterise the main languages taught in British secondary schools, produces a language distance of major proportions which confronts English speaking learners from the start of their study and remains '*the most enduring difficulty for an English speaker learning French ... noun gender'* (Farrington 1986:87). The same can be said of the other European languages taught in British schools.

Concepts that are absent in the mother tongue have been proved over and over again by linguistic research to be difficult areas of language to master. '*It seems to be far more difficult to remember to put things in (a language) than it does to leave things out*' (Wilkins 1972:194). Because no similar cognitive concept exists, learners have first to understand or at least recognise the new concept before they can begin to learn it. Because no comparable cognitive procedure exists in the mother tongue, a cognitive process has to be created *a priori*.

Current research in neuroscience is revealing to us just how the brain functions. The advent of machines such as CAT scanners, PET, MRI and MEG[1] allow scientists to watch the brain at work. Although the final secrets are still a long way off being learnt, much can be stated with certainty about how cognitive procedures are established.

> *We know that everyday experience triggers neuronal development... which means that the more areas of the brain are stimulated and used, the more neuronal pathways and networks are established.* (Winkley 1999)

From birth we lose neurons at an alarming rate; those that we retain are those that we need to interact with our environment. The development that experience causes in our brain is one of connection.

> *Experience sculptures the brain through patterns of connections. After a few repetitions of cell groups firing together, they tend to team up. This is called Hebbian learning.... when two connected neurones have been triggered together on several occasions, the cells and synapses between them change chemically, so that when one fires, it will be a stronger trigger for the other.* (Winkley 1999)

Connections are not made singly or in a linear way. The brain receiving new input, and having no immediate and obvious pathway to deal with it, creates a multitude of connections (axons) in all directions and at all levels, some random, some seeking out existing parallel or similar neural networks; this is the initial stage of learning – the stage at which understanding still has not taken place, where the information being received is still chaotic. Connections made may be as a result of half understood concepts given to the student by the teacher or hypotheses created by the student with reference to any knowledge that he/she thinks might be relevant. They might be useful, they might be useless.

More exposure to the experience, i.e. repetition or reinforcement, is required before the brain can create order out of chaos.

> *Those connections that are used more often, because they more aptly help interact with the surroundings, are strengthened. The driving force behind the strengthenings is based on the satisfaction of certain inherited values selected through evolution. For example: light is preferred to dark.* (Edelman 1987)

In pedagogy, the inherited value might be said to be the satisfaction of success or understanding. It is possible too that negative values are in force: random connections that do not promote success are actively avoided and thus minimised until non-existent.

We could go as far as to define learning as *'the biological organisation of new experience'* (Rendall 2000); once the neuronal connections that produce the desired result, whether comprehension or skill, are in place and can be relied on to fire accurately whenever called upon, then Hebbian learning has taken place. *'Neurons that fire together, wire together'* (Edelman 2000). Neuronal selection has been fixed. It is now a matter of using that new pathway on a regular basis, because there is one more fact to be taken into consideration.

> *Our brain connections are in a constant, restless state, reflecting our individual experiences. It's a jungle in there: your brain operates on a ruthless use it or lose it principle* (Greenfield 1999).

In order for learning to take place, the brain must be given the opportunity to:
- create order out of chaos;
- from the welter of new random connections, create patterns of connections that produce set value results of success and, though this is less certain, learn to avoid those patterns that produce failure;
- to hone these connections until a fixed pattern emerges which can be relied on to produce the same result as and when required;
- to re-visit these fixed patterns or neural pathways.

In order for this to happen, there must be:
- repetition within a short space of time;

- clear and immediate indicators of success or failure;
- opportunity to use the knowledge or skill that results.

This set of criteria for learning provides us with a yardstick with which to measure the pedagogic usefulness of methodology. And this is where the computer and its programmable capacity comes in. Computers have been used in secondary education for less than twenty years. Yet their potential was recognised early on:

> *The computer is interactive. The student responds and gets instant feedback: either positive reinforcement or notification of a mistake. The computer is capable of error analysis: identification and explanation of the source of error, which in turn allows for self-correction. And of course (it) is inhumanly patient with the student, who may go over material as much as he/she needs.* (Underwood 1988)

Compare these characteristics with the learning requirements of the brain and it would seem that the computer could be an ideal tool with which to provide precisely the environment that is needed – so long as the program is designed to achieve these criteria. Over sophistication of computer programming could lead to loss of cognitive activity on the part of the student. What is important is not what the computer itself does, but what it makes the pupil do and whether that experience of action/interaction either creates or reinforces cognitive patterning in the brain.

Modern foreign language learning offers an excellent research basis to investigate whether these claims can be upheld. Unlike other curriculum subjects, MFL teachers can predict a lack of knowledge and experience in certain areas: for example, in many areas of the country most, if not all, pupils are likely to be monolingual English speakers. This will mean that pupils arrive in their first foreign language lesson with no ready-made and automated cognitive procedure to deal with the concept of gender or gender agreement as understood and required by French or German. For them the seemingly random gender allocation to nouns makes little or no sense. They have to have their attention drawn to the importance of gender and adjective agreement and they must constantly be reminded to learn new nouns with an article clearly marking gender.

In the early years of IT and secondary education I chanced upon a program that had been designed by Russel Wills of Dundee for ESL teaching. He called it *Word Sequencing*. The teacher enters a series of unambiguous sentences, which the computer then jumbles up in turn along a horizontal plane; the pupil using two sets of keys has to arrange the words into the correct order. This seemingly simple program was to have far reaching effects on my pupils and their learning.

While I was teaching, I had no time to pursue a systematic study of the effects on learning of any of the IT programs I was using: experience showed that extraordinary advances were being made by those groups who had regular access to the computer network; it showed in their more than usually rapid progress; it was evident in the accuracy and extent of their productive work after two years of learning. But there was no time to isolate whether or not this was because of the computer exercises or because of increased motivation generated by using computers. It may have been as a result of new course books. They may have been a particularly responsive group of pupils.

It was not until 1996 that I was able to begin a long term observation and recording of pupils using this program. A group of twelve pupils was selected from a class of 24 in a three-form entry rural comprehensive. Two pupils with high Cognitive Abilities Test[2] (CAT) scores were balanced by two pupils with low scores. To this were added two with average scores, three more were chosen from the grades above and below the average score.

For the next three years I attempted to integrate computer assisted learning on a regular basis – c. 30 minutes a week out of two hours of French. One difference between this study and my own practice ten years earlier became immediately apparent – the amount of vocabulary, the breadth of structure and the rapidity with which topics were covered in no way compared with the more leisurely pace of the previous decade. As a result we were not able to systematically keep up with vocabulary learning. New words could be practised in the week of learning and reinforced the next week, but by the third week pupils would already be on a new topic and a new set of vocabulary was needing to be tackled. It was not quite the same for grammatical structure, however, the bases remained much the same over the topics: gender, articles and adjective agreements; verb endings and tenses; pronouns; possession, etc. It was soon clear that concentrating on essential grammatical structures and characteristics would probably prove more successful in the long run.

Within three weeks of starting French the computer group was practising gender matching using *Word Sequencing*. Pairs of nouns were entered into the program; the computer jumbled them up – see Figure 1.1; pupils had to sort them back into the correct pairing. A capital letter gave away the first word.

sentence 1	compas	une	calculette	et	Un
sentence 2	règle	et	Une	un	bic
sentence 3	feutres	surligneur	Des	un	et
sentence 4	un	et	trousse	Une	sac

Figure 1.1: Jumbled sentences in Word Sequencing

Not surprisingly the first set of results was not particularly good – the efforts were chaotic and inconsistent. Despite oral/aural backup (when I read the correct solution aloud to them) at this early stage, before ears and eyes could match sound and spelling, even such a simple task proved difficult.

The results for the 26 September 1996 are shown in Figure 1.2: the headings refer to:

Group number = the pupils were working in pairs: one person was absent so group 4 comprised just one pupil;

Attempt number = the number of exercises attempted; it was clear from visual observation that some groups, still not trained in writing down their results, attempted more exercises than just the single result entered;

Errors = the number of times the group pressed the FINISH key believing they had correctly sorted the jumble when in fact there were mistakes in the sorting;

the number of sentences/pairings completed correctly: there were thirteen sentences/pairings in this first exercise;

the time taken to achieve 13/13 correct exercise: pupils entered a maximum time of ten minutes. When this ran out, the exercise was automatically terminated and the group would start again.

Group	attempt no.	errors	number of sentences	time taken
1	1	8	5/13	10 minutes
	2	15	4/13	10 minutes
2	1	0	13/13	5.19 mins
	2	1	13/13	4.6 mins
3	1	6	13/13	5.5 mins
	2	7	13/13	5.9 mins
4	1	11	4/13	10 mins
5	1	10	13/13	7.6 mins
6	1	not noted	13/13	6.9

Figure 1.2: Results for 26 September 1996

The average time taken to achieve each single sentence correctly was 7.3 minutes. By the beginning of November of the same term adjectives had been learnt and adjective agreement could be added to the structure, so that exercise JS6b appeared as in Figure 1.3.

sentence 1	rouge	rouges	ciseaux	et	Un	des	crayon
sentence 2	un	Une	et	règle	vert	verte	crayon
sentence 3	bleue	une	sac	et	calculette	Un	bleu
sentence 4	et	noire	Un	une	feutre	noir	règle

Figure 1.3: Exercise JS6b

Again the results, to start with, were inconsistent, some groups managing to complete all thirteen, others barely able to make a single pair match correctly. But what is remarkable is the progress made by all groups over the next three lessons. By 21 November the results had changed dramatically. Over that month the pupils, having repeated the same exercise over three thirty-minute lessons, had developed strategies for dealing with the jumbled information and could sort it out correctly. The results are shown in Figure 1.4.

Some groups had by now chosen to split and pupils were working on their own: these are numbered 1a & 1b etc.

Group	attempt	errors	number of sentences	time taken
1a	7 Nov 1	0	0	10 mins
	2	0	0	10 mins
	14 Nov 1	18	2	10 mins
	2	6	4	10 mins
	21 Nov 1	13	5	10 mins
	2	6	5	10 mins
1b	7 Nov 1	3	1	10 mins
	2	6	7	10 mins
	14 Nov 1	7	6	10 mins
	2	12	6	10 mins
	21 Nov 1	12	11	10 mins
	2	11	12	10 mins
2	7 Nov 1	1	11	10 mins
	2	3	13	6.4 mins
	3	0	13	6.1 mins
	14 Nov	moved to different	file	
	21 Nov 1	1	13	5.1 mins
3a	7 Nov 1	3	10/10 (pupil sets no.)	10 mins
	2	0	10/10	6.5 mins
	14 Nov 1	moved to different	file	
	21 Nov 1	5	13	7.8
	2	7	13	7.6
	3	0	13	4.1
3b	7 Nov 1	7	3	10 mins
	2	9	7	10 mins
	14 Nov 1	9	10	10 mins
		4	13	8.5 mins
		0	13	6.1 mins
	21 Nov 1	6	13	7 mins
		2	13	6.1 mins

Figure 1.4: Results for the 21 November 1996

Even the pupil 1a had progressed. Working alone for the first time on 7 November, she sat looking blankly at the screen, unable to move, react or even touch a key. Despite the fact that for the first ten minutes there would have been oral/aural backup, she was totally unable to cope with the activity. Within three weeks she was not only working and thinking for herself, but was able to produce five correct sentences with only six errors. For her personally this was major progress.

Groups 2 and 3a seemed to cope from the first lesson onwards and, despite moving onto a different file in between times, when they returned to the file on the 21st they retained their high rate of success: low error scores which decrease to nil; all sentences/pairings completed; increasingly faster rates of completion.

Obviously, success with an activity repeated over such a short time could be the result of familiarity with the content or a short-term memory strategy. So the real test comes later. It comprises two elements:

Repeating the same file at a much later date. Have they retained strategies for dealing with this activity? Can they maintain their previous scores? Can they better their previous scores?

Can they transfer their new strategies into knowledge? i.e. can they transfer this accuracy into free, unprompted production in either speaking or writing?

The scores for the same file repeated twelve months later on 12 December 1997 are presented in Figure 1.5.

By this time Group 2 had separated and were working individually.

3a was absent.

1b had paired up with a new partner.

*2b attempt 4 – stayed behind during break to finish: hence the extra time total.

Once a pupil or a group had succeeded with a zero error score, they moved on to a different exercise.

Group	attempt	errors	number of sentences	time taken
1a	1	11	1	10 mins
	2	13	5	12 (pupil sets clock)
1b	1	4	13	9.8 mins
	2	0	13	5 mins
2a	1	0	13	4.3 mins
2b	1	21	3	10 mins
	2	21	6	10mins
	3	13	8	10 mins
	4	3	13	7.3 mins *
3b	1	18	13	8.3 mins
	2	1	13	5.8 mins
	3	0	13	4.1 mins

Figure 1.5: Results from 12 December 1997

It would seem that for the majority of the pupils the cognitive pathways, the coping strategies, whatever one likes to call the methods by which these pupils achieved accuracy in these activities, were either immediately to hand (groups 1b &2a) or could be recalled within one or two attempts (groups 2b & 3b) and that even 1a managed to equal her previous year's score by the second attempt – even though her first attempt was pretty disastrous.

As for the second element, the transfer into productive knowledge, this took longer to appear. The evidence of actual transfer of thinking skills was not significantly noticeable in the free writing assessments until late in Year 8, and then more particularly in Year 9.

In the final written task of this three-year observation (Easter 1999), the spontaneous use of adjectives could be summed up by the following results. The task involved pupils being given a blank sheet of paper and asked to write as much as they could about themselves in French. This task had been set at the end of Year 7 and then twice a year in Years 8 and 9, so pupils were well used to it.

In Figures 1.6 to 1.8 the names along the top row indicate the different classes in the year group:

JS1– the computer group, down to 10 people on the test day;

JS2 – the other 13 people in the same class;
RC – another class totalling 22 out of the normal 28 pupils that day;
GS – the third class in the year, here totalling 15 pupils only as the other 8 in the class were all designated special needs (SN) and as such their results have been removed to avoid an extreme imbalance of results.

The results in Figure 1.6 show the computer group JS1 achieving slightly less good results than the class GS but significantly better results than the other two JS2 and RC.

	JS1	%	JS2	%	RC	%	GS	%
using more than 8 adjectives	3	30%	3	23.0%	2	9.0%	5	33.3%
using 5—8 adjectives	1	10%	2	15.3%	1	4.5%	4	26.6%
using 3—5 adjectives	3	30%	1	7.6%	2	9.0%	2	13.3%
using 1—3 adjectives	1	10%	3	23.0%	7	31.8%	3	20.0%
using no adjectives	2	20%	4	30.7%	10	45.4 %	1	6.6%

Figure 1.6: Written task Easter 1999 – Use of adjectives by number

Marking the use of the adjectives was necessarily complicated. Correct position and correct agreement were obviously essential, but what about inconsistent use of either? Some pupils used French and English adjectives seemingly at random. Finally it seemed that the only way was to categorise under the following main headings:

- adjectives in the target language only;
- adjectives in the target language and English;
- adjectives only in English.

In Figure 1.7 we see JS1, the computer group, edging its way in front of GS by a fraction. It could be argued that the removal from GS of all pupils designated SN has created an imbalance in favour of the more able and that this is borne out by this very low percentage in the *used no adjectives* category.

	JS1	%	JS2	%	RC	%	GS	%
adjectives in the TL only	7	70%	6	46%	10	45.3%	10	66.6%
adjectives in the TL & English	0	—	2	15.2 %	0	—	4	26.6%
adjectives in English	1	10%	1	7.6%	2	9%	0	—
no adjectives	2	20%	4	30.7%	10	45.5%	1	6.6%

Figure 1.7: Written task Easter 1999 – Use of adjectives by language

Each of the two first categories above were then given the following sub-headings;

- all correct
- randomly applied
- masculine form only (a common enough occurrence to warrant a sub-heading)

Of the pupils using adjectives in the target language only, the results are shown in Figure 1.8.

	JS 1	%	JS 2	%	RC	%	GS	%
adjectives all correct	1	10%	0	–	0	–	0	–
adjectives randomly applied	3	30%	4	30.7%	6	27.2%	7	46.6%
adjectives in masc singular only	3	30%	2	15.3%	4	18.1%	3	20%
total %		70%		46%		45.3%		66.6%

Figure 1.8: Written task Easter 1999 – Use of adjectives by accuracy

So, after three years of MFL learning, only one pupil was able to place and agree French adjectives correctly and she was a member of the computer group. Although frequency of use was not used as a measure, it is interesting to note that she had used 22 adjectives; the next highest number came from a pupil in GS who had used sixteen.

It should be noted when comparing the above results that the difference in the average CAT scores across the groups as shown in Figure 1.9 is significant and adds to the interpretation of the results.

Form	JS1	JS2	RC	GS (all)	GS (minus 8)
1996 Year 7	92	99	97	95	104.5
1997 Year 8	98	98	99	96.6	104.8

Figure 1.9: CAT scores

In the light of these, the computer group JS1 can be seen to be performing exceptionally well for their CAT average. It was to be expected that GS would outperform the other classes, having maintained a higher CAT average over the Key Stage. That JS1 should pip them at the post (70% against 66.6%) although there is a difference of almost seven points in their respective CAT averages, was both unexpected and gratifying.

The leap in JS1's CAT score between Year 7 & Year 8 is quite remarkable. It is hoped that time will allow for a further comparison with scores from the end of KS3.

So what conclusions can be drawn? Certainly in the results from November 1996 it is possible to watch pupils learning: they move within a space of weeks from being unable to work out the correct order for jumbled words to, not just getting them right, but, as video recording of Group 1b's computer shows, getting the words, move for move, in the correct sequential order, i.e. placing the article with the capital letter first and then going straight for the correct noun and positioning it after the article, then the correct adjective, etc. The high incidence of errors shown for 1b relates to a single sentence that caused repeated problems, rather than to a spread of problems across the exercise.

To be able to move faultlessly to the next word implies that the mind controlling the hand appears to be anticipating the correct sentence order, which in turn implies that the correct sentence order appears now to be stored somewhere in the brain. When asked why they think their solution is correct, before they check with the computer program, most pupils will reply *'It sounds right'*. When it is pointed out to them that they have not spoken, neither has the computer, they tap their heads and say *'It sounds right in here'*.

It would appear that the most basic characteristics of a computer program – its ability to check step by step; its ability to feedback instantly on error or success; its constant availability in the same form; the possibility of repeating short exercises over and over again within a short space of time – all these appear to enable pupils to accelerate the creation of new cognitive or neural pathways. What in normal everyday life living in France would take the ears and the brain weeks, maybe months, to assimilate, can be experienced, and repeatedly practised, at will on a computer. In so doing, mistakes and errors are eliminated by the process in the brain that labels input with positive or negative value and strengthens those pathways that offer success and either deliberately avoids those which lead to failure or learns to connect certain pathways with warnings of failure.

The fact that the brightest and best learners appear to have already developed strategies for coping is not surprising. Precisely because they are bright and the best learners, they will have learnt well straightaway in the classroom. What they achieve from these computer programs is the possibility of honing their skills to automaticity. For others, at the other end of the learning scale, the individual input required by the computer ensures their participation – for some a shock after years of trained idleness in class. Not all pupils gain maximum benefit from such exercises, but all pupils do improve and, as the final results show, make improvement beyond average expectations.

That this process – the transfer from practice to production – is slow and can take years before it shows up in spontaneous work, should not surprise teachers, though it may come as something of a shock to pupils, few of whom anticipate the difficulties they are likely to face in learning a second language. The gap between receptive and productive competence is wide in most subjects, but never more so than when assessing language skills – even in one's own mother tongue. This fact reinforces the conclusion highlighted here: that practice of any one structure must continue weeks and months past its initial introduction, if pupils are to make it their own.

The final conclusion to be drawn from the above report is perhaps the most unexpected: that computer programs do not have to be sophisticated, all-singing all-dancing multimedia in order to have an effect on pupils' learning. This is a simple program – yet it works and it works on many levels: from such early gender pairings as illustrated here to truly foreign grammar structures tackled by sixth formers. Try sorting out *lui donné ne Je pas le ai* without having developed an internal ear for the finished sentence. Watch Year 9 pupils struggling to divine the difference between *nuits C' pour est de combien?* And *nuit C' pour est combien une?*

Stephen Wolfram has suggested that '*the language of science of the future will be patterns not equations'*. Talking about the patterns in his soon to be published book *A new kind of science* he says:

> *One might have thought – I know I did – that with simple rules one could only make simple patterns.... Even though it starts off from just one black cell, applying the same simple rule over and over again makes (cellular automaton) rule 30 produce amazingly complex patterns.*

It would seem that this simple computer program has a similar effect on the brain. By the repeated sorting of like structures, the brain is able to create strategies for success and can learn to avoid those that fail. By revisiting the same or similar exercises on a frequent basis, the brain strengthens and hones the neural pathways established until they become automatic, subliminal activities – by which time all the pupil knows is that the language springs to mind unbidden.

After three years of observation I cannot say that any of the pupils had reached the unconscious state of automaticity, but some of them were well on their way. It will need more time and more practice, but for a small group of twelve pupils it may well take less time and practice, having had the opportunity of working with such a computer program.

Bibliography

Corder S P, 'Learner language and teacher talk' in *Audio-visual language journal*, Vol 16: 1, (1978)

Edelman G, *Brain, mind and the society at the millennium*, public debate, Brighton (2000)

Edelman G, *Neural Darwinism: The theory of neuronal group selection.* (New York: Basic Books, 1987)

Farrington B, 'Computer assisted learning or computer inhibited learning' in Cameron K, W Dodd &. S Rahtz (eds) *Computers and Modern Language Studies* (Ellis Howood 1986)

Greenfield S, Richard Dimbleby lecture (1999)

Rendall H, *Modern foreign languages: Effective grammar* (Folens, 2000)

Ringbom H, *The role of the first language in foreign language learning* (Multilingual Matters, 1989)

Underwood J, *CALL in language technology* (1988)

Wilkins D A, *Linguistics in language teaching* (Edward Arnold, 1972)

Winkley Sir David, 1999 TES/Keele lecture

Wolfram S, 'The universe in black and white' *The Daily Telegraph* 14 January 1999[3]

Notes

1 CAT = computerised axial tomography scanners : PET = positron emission tomography : MRI = magnetic resonance imaging and MEG = magnetoencephalography

2 Information on CAT available from the NFER-Nelson website: www.nfer-nelson.co.uk/cat/index.htm

3 Available on Electronic Telegraph website

Chapter 2

ICT and community languages: Insights from a web publishing project

Jim Anderson

Introduction

Although there have been numerous investigations into the effects of ICT in relation to first and second languages (Warschauer and Healey 1998), the vast majority of these focus on high status European languages – English, French, German, Spanish – written in Roman script. This is not surprising when one considers that computer technology was developed to a large extent in the United States for an English speaking *clientele* and that its use in the developing world, although growing rapidly, still lags far behind that in industrialised countries. Nevertheless, a number of studies going back some ten years have identified positive outcomes from the introduction of multilingual word processing packages (including languages in Arabic and Indic scripts) in UK schools. A recent investigation (Chana, Edwards and Walker 1998), looking at the effects of introducing an Urdu word processing package at a primary school in Reading, highlights the benefits in terms of:

- language status and recognition of the expertise of the bilingual children;
- Pakistani children's increased confidence in the development of their writing and computer skills;
- English children's interest in learning to speak, read and write in Urdu;
- increased involvement of Pakistani parents in supporting their children's learning.

Building on this work, the study which forms the focus of this chapter set out to investigate the effects of various uses of ICT within an Urdu and Bengali web publishing project. The study took place at Plashet School, a secondary girls' comprehensive in the London Borough of Newham. The vast majority of students at the school are of Asian background and are bilingual or multilingual. As well as French, Urdu and Bengali are offered on the timetable.

The project involved two Year 9 classes studying Urdu and Bengali and was planned and implemented collaboratively between the class teachers, the ICT coordinator and myself. Students' levels of proficiency in Urdu/Bengali varied widely within the classes and this was particularly the case with regard to literacy. All students had acquired basic ICT skills and had been introduced to word processing in Urdu and Bengali during the year of the project. Some students had also learnt about web page design within their ICT lessons.

The project took place in the second half of the Summer Term and was timed to tie in with the school's Year 9 Arts Week. The theme chosen for the week was *regeneration* and students were expected to select topics related to this theme. The most popular of these were fashion, films and celebrations with students contrasting old and new and reflecting Eastern and Western influences and perspectives.

An important motive behind the interest shown by the Urdu and Bengali teachers in this project was the desire to foster greater student independence. Thus whole class teacher input was kept to a minimum and students, working predominantly in self-selected friendship groups, were given a large amount of choice in determining content, structure and style of their web pages.

The framework for carrying out the project, i.e. planning ⇛ researching ⇛ drafting/redrafting of text ⇛ creation of web pages, was one which clearly accorded with a process writing approach (Daiute 1985; Edwards 1998), i.e. one which takes place within a supportive framework in which ideas are generated through discussion and research (oral interaction, reading for information, note-taking) and where the creation and structuring of text is scaffolded and allowed to develop in stages. This kind of shared writing or writers' workshop approach, which incidentally is ideally suited to developing the skills required for coursework, is one where use of ICT can make an invaluable contribution. It means crucially that ICT can become fully integrated within the process of teaching and learning rather than being seen as a one-off activity.

Stages within the project

With regard to the project under discussion here, figure 2.1 sets out the role played by ICT at successive stages.

	Stage in project	ICT contribution
A	Planning	• World Wide Web audience and implications for register and genre • Parameters for structure (tree diagram)
B	Researching	• Access to up-to-date information on the Web from sources worldwide
		• Spreadsheet software for recording and analysis of survey information
C	Drafting/Redrafting	• Word processing to facilitate drafting/redrafting of work and to enhance presentation • Non-linear writing/reading framework (hypertext option)
D	Creating web pages	• Multimedia options for conveying information and ideas • Desktop publishing software (+ digital camera and scanner) as creative tool, supporting individual expression, maximising visual impact, encouraging collaboration

Figure 2.1: Contribution of ICT at four stages within the project

As we move on now to look more closely at each of these stages, it will become increasingly clear how, throughout the project, use of ICT was instrumental in shaping both purpose and means. It will also become apparent why students found the possibilities that were opened up for them so stimulating and empowering.

Planning

Writing is made simpler and more meaningful when there is a real audience (Daiute 1985). Within the context of this project it was striking how positive students' response was from the outset to the notion of publishing on the Web and how attuned they were to the multimodal possibilities of the medium. Beyond any novelty effect there was a real sense of being involved in something important and exciting. It would mean that their work could be viewed not only by teachers, family, friends in their local community, but across the UK and indeed even in Pakistan and Bangladesh. As Abbott (1998) explains, the Internet has made huge inroads into youth culture in recent years, both in the areas of study and leisure, and this is no doubt part of its appeal.

Following a whole class brainstorming activity when teachers assisted students in developing initial ideas and fed in some key language, students set about their planning in groups. They were encouraged to think not just about aims and content, but also about how they were going to make their work relevant and interesting for people who would be visiting the website. Their discussions reflected the seriousness with which they regarded both what they had to say about their topics and who their potential audience might be. In particular, they clearly valued the way the project allowed them to assert aspects of their culture and identity, including both Asian and Western influences.

As part of their planning related to awareness of audience, groups were also encouraged to think about aspects of register and style. They were aware that a formal essay writing approach would not be appropriate if they wanted to interest young people. It had to be more like a magazine – chatty, informal with a strong visual element. They wished to use both Urdu/Bengali and English on their pages. They would introduce themselves and write something about their school. There would be short descriptive texts supported by images. There would be reports of surveys carried out contrasting views across older and younger generations. There would be interviews, quizzes and poetry.

An important element within the planning stage was ensuring that students were clear both about the hierarchical structure underlying the organization of pages and also about the navigational flexibility and freedom which they could create for the reader by means of hyperlinks both within their own set of pages, but also beyond these to other websites. Some students in each class had already gained a good understanding of these points from ICT lessons and they took on responsibility for designing an overall structure. An interesting point to emerge from observing individual groups planning was how the need to think in terms of web pages and what material might be presented on each page helped in terms of categorising and organising ideas as well as overall coherence.

Researching

A major issue for teachers of Community Languages in the UK has long been the lack of appropriate resources (Molteno 1986). Thus an important area of investigation within the project was to examine the potential of the Web as a source of up-to-date authentic material in Urdu and Bengali. In starting to search for relevant sites relating to the Indian subcontinent, it is immediately striking how much material is in English. There are various reasons for this, not least the fact that since independence English has remained a lingua franca in the region as well as being the international language of commerce. Limitations created by non-Roman fonts have also played a part (Felix 1998).

However, although many sites students visited were in English, both they and the class teachers were convinced that visiting the sites was useful from the point of view of obtaining information and stimulating ideas. The following are some of their comments:

> *It helped me to research on my topic (fashion) and on Asian clothing, jewellery, hairstyles, make-up, etc.*
>
> *I think it is very useful because you can connect with countries where most people speak Urdu.*

> *It is very useful because you can get to find out about all the things that are going on. It's like giving you information about the main things that people are interested in.*
>
> *Very useful because there is a wide range of choices and you learn a lot of teachings on culture.*
>
> *It helps in reading because you can read other people's websites.*

It emerged that some students made regular use of the Web to research topics in other subject areas and so knew how to go about searches and to navigate within and between websites. Those who were new to the Web quickly picked up basic search and navigational skills. Useful starting points were sites which provided lists of links, for example[1]:

> The Pak Ranks (lists over seven hundred sites with content ranging from government to Lollywood, Pakistan's version of Bollywood);
>
> Pakistan – Land of the Pure (very comprehensive, includes Urdu newspapers);
>
> U-hoo!!! – Urdu's answer to Yahoo! (focus on Urdu language, poetry, computer software);
>
> Virtual Bangladesh (covers every aspect of life and culture in Bangladesh);
>
> West Bengal (official site of West Bengal);
>
> Club India Internet Services (includes Asian fashion with section on The Designer Collections from London Fashions);

It is not hard to see the attraction of websites of this type. As Luke (2000:87) points out:

> *The multimodal and iconographic nature of the World Wide Web and CD-ROMs appeals to learners of all ages by mediating the difficulty and apprehension many first and second language learners often have.*

They are not dealing with dry text in what might be out-of-date publications. Comprehension is supported by strong audiovisual elements (images, recordings, video clips) and hyperlinking encourages more flexible and interactive reading – skimming for gist, scanning for key markers (leading on to closer examination of a particular section/web page), switching back and forth between pages. This may account for the large amounts of time that many students devoted to searching the Web outside lessons. Teachers commented on how much pupils had found out by themselves through their searches. A good example of this emerged in relation to Mehndi design, which one group of students, through visiting *The Art of Mehndi* website, had been inspired to make a focus in their own work.

For pedagogical as well as other reasons (Pachler and Williams 1999), it is important that students acquire a focused and critical stance in the way they view websites and the information contained in them. In this project, students were encouraged to compare different websites on the basis of specific criteria and to decide which they would wish to recommend and provide hyperlinks to from their own web pages. It is also important to be aware that some websites contain material which might be considered unsuitable by parents if not by teachers themselves. In this regard, it is helpful if there is a whole school policy on use of the Internet.

Drafting/redrafting

Although many students involved in this project were fluent orally in Urdu or Bengali when they arrived at Plashet School, literacy skills were very limited. Thus they had to face the challenge of learning to operate in a new script and of familiarising themselves with a new set of writing conventions. On top of this, when it came to word processing, they had to learn a new system for keying in text. An important issue here is the system adopted by the school as some are far more user-friendly than others[2]. In relation to this project, it is important to bear in mind that students had had limited experience of using the Urdu/Bengali word processing packages and that the system adopted for keying in text was not the most user-friendly one.

The classes were taken to computer rooms to work on their texts after initial planning and research had taken place and most students arrived with handwritten notes in Urdu/Bengali which they began by typing up and then expanded. In some groups one or two students would take main responsibility for typing, in others typing in Urdu/Bengali would be assigned to one pair of students, while typing in English was assigned to another. Sometimes students took the typing in turns. The project confirmed findings from previous studies (Atkinson 1992; Crook 1994) that the public nature of writing at the computer encourages collaborative learning. Students took a real interest in the progress of each other's writing, turned to each other for help with language (spellings in particular) as well as technical questions and provided moral support when disaster struck in the form of work being lost due to faults on the network and/or forgetting to save work. During sessions in the computer room, teachers circulated around the class discussing work with the students, suggesting improvements and assisting them with difficulties related to the keyboard. A frequent suggestion made was that students should select a larger font size in order to be able to read the script more easily and indeed this was something that students also suggested to each other.

The fact that, in spite of many difficulties and frustrations, students persevered with word processing and returned to the computer rooms in their lunch hour and after school to continue work may be attributed partly to their high levels of motivation with regard to this project. However, there was evidence of a strong conviction amongst the vast majority of students that word processing assisted their writing. A wide range of reasons were given for this and they reflect similar findings in a number of other studies of students writing in first and second languages.

Some related to clarity ('... *identifying letters, ... makes work easier to read*') and acquiring a better understanding of sentence construction ('*I can see what words go into what, ... now I know how to join sentences and Urdu makes more sense to me*'). Possibly partly due to this greater clarity some pupils felt it assisted memorisation ('... *learning spellings, ... remembering words and how to rewrite them*'). For many, ease of correction was an important factor ('... *when I make mistakes it helps me correct them rather than writing them again and again, It just makes it faster and if you make spelling mistakes, the computer takes it out for you*') as was neatness and overall presentation ('... *looks good, ...makes your writing neat*'). Several students pointed out that using a computer supported their learning because it made writing more enjoyable ('*It encourages you to do more work because it's fun typing, ...you are learning computer skills as well and it is easier to remember*'). Some students were also aware that they would be able to word process their GCSE coursework in Urdu/Bengali and they felt that this would be an advantage for them.

Teachers were also strongly of the view that word processing supported students' writing. For beginners they felt that the advantage lay particularly in the recognition of letter shapes and the formation of words and simple sentences. For students with more advanced skills it was to do with the way in which the computer supported drafting and redrafting and thus encouraged greater creativity and risk taking.

In spite of these very positive views expressed by both students and teachers towards word processing in this project, some concerns were also raised. A number of students commented on difficulties in keying in text and it was evident from observation what a slow and laborious process it was for many of them.

The issue of input method has already been raised, but, irrespective of this, it is increasingly being recognised (Pennington, 1996) that a process of training and familiarisation needs to take place before students are able to benefit fully from the facilities that the word processor provides. It is, in fact, only when the processes involved in operating the software have become more or less automatic and the writer is released from the need to attend to the mechanics of text production that it becomes possible to focus more intensively on the finer aspects of composition such as structuring and elaboration of ideas. This might explain why, for most students, redrafting took place at the micro level of corrections to spelling and grammar with some minor additions and deletions (i.e. text editing) rather than at the macro level of reconfiguration in which direction and organization of ideas are developed at the keyboard as part of an organic process (i.e. text revision). However, this kind of global approach may also be dependent on students having reached a certain level in their general writing skills.

Creating web pages

Although the drafting of text represented a clear phase within this project, students were aware from the outset that their end product would be one which would draw on the multiple creative possibilities of multimedia both in terms of content and of organization. In many respects, this shift from linear to multidimensional thinking was not new for them. In projects carried out from primary school onwards – whether resulting in magazines, displays or dramatised presentations – students learn to draw on and integrate different media. The skills and processes involved in desktop publishing projects in particular are in many ways similar.

As students began creating their web pages, they were reminded of several key points:

- the importance of designing pages in such a way as to engage audience interest;
- the need to be clear about overall structure, i.e. what levels of importance within the hierarchical system would be assigned to different pages;
- the need to facilitate navigation within the web pages through careful design of the Home Page and through creating appropriate links;
- the limited amount of time available.

Here, as throughout the project, it was striking how well students worked together, drawing on each other's interests and expertise in relation to content, language and images and use of technology. Initially students planned to copy images from other websites or to scan in pictures from magazines and newspapers as illustrations on their pages, but the time it might have taken to obtain copyright permission made this impractical. Thus students covering fashion decided to use the digital camera to take pictures of each other modelling different clothes, shoes, jewellery, hairstyles and make-up and to select the best of these images for their web pages. The school's digital camera was also used to produce other images that students wished to include. As well as this photographic material, some students created drawings which were scanned into the web pages. The fact that students themselves created most of the images used on the web pages, apart from the obvious enjoyment they derived from this, meant that their sense of personal involvement in, and therefore ownership of, the final product was greatly enhanced.

Observation of students discussing their work in progress revealed the thought and energy that went into the creation of each web page. Class teachers commented on the stimulus the project provided for all students, irrespective of attainment level, to produce original and interesting work. However, as previously mentioned, they also hoped that the project would encourage greater independence and creativity, particularly as far as the higher attaining students were concerned. This had been identified as a priority of the department in relation to meeting National Curriculum requirements and was also part of a whole school agenda to provide greater challenge for gifted and talented students.

Nevertheless, the teachers were genuinely surprised by the range and quality of work produced as well as by the careful planning that had gone into creation of the web pages. A point particularly stressed was how much of the work students had done entirely on their own[3].

Moving on

In many respects the investigation supports findings from previous research in terms of benefits and issues involved in CALL. It also demonstrates, however, how in the context of the learning and teaching of community languages there are important additional dimensions to be taken into consideration. These have to do with status and motivation, self-expression and identity, independence and creativity as well as practical issues involved in working with non-Roman fonts. If schools are seriously to address issues around inclusion highlighted in the revised National Curriculum documents (1999), then the importance of these dimensions has to be recognised and built into planning.

At the same time, there is a need for further research to explore more precisely how use of ICT can most effectively be built into existing pedagogical approaches to the learning and teaching of community languages. Relevant questions would include:

At what stage is it most appropriate to begin introducing word processing? (This may vary between languages)

What types of word processing software are most appropriate for students at different stages of literacy development?

How can students be trained to make most effective use of the word processor so that more flexible and creative approaches to the writing process are encouraged?

In what ways can authentic material downloaded from the Web (in community languages/in English) be most effectively exploited at different stages in students' learning to develop language skills and intercultural understanding?

What skills and understandings do students need to acquire to use the Web efficiently and critically in their learning?

How should web pages created by students be evaluated?

How can the audience factor in web publishing, identified in this project, be extended through, for example, e-mail links with schools in target communities in the UK/worldwide?

How can the use of ICT be exploited to enable students to become more independent as learners? (This is of particular relevance where classes take place only once a week as in the case of most voluntary community-run schools)

Acknowledgements

I would like to extend my thanks to the Headteacher at Plashet School, Mrs B. Nasir for allowing this study to take place and to colleagues involved in this project for their commitment and support. In particular I am grateful to Mrs T. Mirza (Urdu specialist, Head of Community languages), Mr M. Mazed (Bengali specialist) and Ms M. Woodhead (Head of ICT). I would also like to thank the students in the two Year 9 classes that took part in the project. Their enthusiasm and commitment was impressive. Finally, I am grateful to the WELL (Web Enhanced Language Learning) Project supported by FDTL (Fund for the Development of Teaching and Learning) for its interest in and support of this study.

Bibliography

Abbott C, 'Making connections: Young people and the Internet' in Sefton-Green (ed.) *Digital diversions: Youth culture in the age of multimedia.* (UCL Press, 1998)

Atkinson T, 'Le hamster a mangé mon pneu: creative writing and IT' in *Language learning journal* No.6: 68–70 (1992)

Chana U, V Edwards and S Walker, 'Hidden resources; multilingual word processing in the primary school' in *Race, ethnicity and education,* Vol 1: No. 1, (1998)

Crook C, *Computers and the collaborative experience of learning* (Routledge, 1994)

Daiute C, *Writing and computers.* (Reading, Mass.: Addison-Wesley, 1985)

Edwards V, *The power of Babel: Teaching and learning in multilingual classrooms* (Trentham Books, 1998)

Felix U, *Virtual language learning – finding the gems among the pebbles* (Melbourne: Language Australia, 1998)

Luke C, 'Cyber-schooling and technological change: Multiliteracies for new times' in Cope B and M Kalantzis (eds.) *Multiliteracies: Literacy learning and the design of social futures.* (Routledge, 2000)

Molteno M, *Teaching Britain's community languages: materials and methods* (CILT, 1986)

Pachler N and L Williams, 'Using the Internet as a teaching and learning tool' in Leask M and N Pachler (eds) *Learning to teach using ICT in the secondary school* (Routledge, 1999)

Pennington M C, 'Writing the natural way: On computer' in *Computer assisted language learning,* Vol 9: No 2–3, 125–142 (1996)

DfEE/QCA, The National Curriculum: Handbook for primary teachers in England (1999)

DfEE/QCA, The National Curriculum: Handbook for secondary teachers in England (1999)

Warschauer M and D Healey, 'Computers and language learning: an overview' in *Language teaching,* Vol 31: 57–71 (1998)

Notes

1 The URLs (at the time of writing) for the sites mentioned are given below.

The Pak Ranks	www.pakranks.com/
Pakistan – Land of the Pure	www.memonics.com/pak/
U-hoo!!!	www.urdustan.com/u-hoo/
Virtual Bangladesh	www.virtualbangladesh.com/
West Bengal	www.westbengal.com/
Club India Internet Services	www.indialog.com/index.htm

2 Options for keying in text:

- to use a clickable on screen keyboard display (the most user-friendly system for beginners, but also very slow to operate)
- to replace the QWERTY keyboard with one dedicated to the language in question (the optimum choice, though relatively expensive)
- to place stickers or a plastic overlay onto the QWERTY keyboard (a cheaper alternative to 2)
- to provide students with a reference sheet showing the distribution of characters based on the QWERTY keyboard (the cheapest, but least desirable option since it involves students in relating one set of keys to another as well as switching between two scripts)

Students may also have to learn procedures for producing different forms of characters. This applies to changes in characters related to position in the word in Urdu and to conjunct characters in Bengali. Some programs actually facilitate these changes. Thus for Urdu, a system of contextual analysis may be built in, automatically selecting the appropriate form of characters according to their position in the word. For Bengali, a system may be built in to achieve automatic conjuncting. Where these systems are not provided, however, a complex series of keyboard operations involving the shift key are required.

3 To view examples of work carried out by students in this project visit the website of the Community Languages Forum, Goldsmiths' College at: www.gold.ac.uk/clf

Chapter 3

Applying new technologies appropriately to foreign handwriting recognition difficulties

David R. Wilson

Modern foreign language (MFL) learners with special educational needs (SEN) often cite copying from teachers' handwriting on the board as their single most daunting experience (McColl 2000). Authentic target language (TL) handwriting is even likelier to challenge these learners in general and students with Specific Learning Difficulties such as Dyslexia in particular (Jameson 1999). The purpose of this chapter is to describe action research into what needs a TL handwriting-challenged student may have and how these needs might be supported in the classroom. My investigation was replicated over several years using Information and Communications Technology (ICT) as a problem-solving instrument of research and teaching. I have divided this chapter into three sections. The first gives background information about the place of school handwriting in our digital age. In the second, I describe my school-based project applying ICT to Year 7 MFL readers' difficulties with authentic handwritten TL texts. The third section lists the principal outcomes of the study, with recommendations for further research and development.

The background

In this section, I describe the wider context of my research and more especially:

- the challenges and conventions associated with the integration of TL cursive scripts into MFL teaching;
- the implications of national primary school handwriting policies and practices at home and abroad;
- the changing relationship between computers and handwriting with particular reference to the human skills of penmanship and keyboarding.

Students routinely ask teachers to read aloud or translate pen-pal letters from abroad. Often the message proves to be couched in very simple idiom, which ought to be intelligible to the recipient. It may even be in English. Further probing usually reveals that the sender's joined handwriting is the main barrier to comprehension.

Now that authentic resources play a key role in the teaching and testing of modern foreign languages, the ability to decode cursive script is a necessity. To qualify for National Curriculum (NC) Level 4 in Reading and Responding, for instance, students must understand short stories and factual texts which are '*printed or clearly handwritten*' (DfEE & QCA 1999).

General Certificate of Secondary Education (GCSE) candidates are particularly likely to encounter a handwritten letter as a reading passage in their MFL examinations. However accessible the language is, they cannot answer questions about its content if all they see is an illegible scrawl. The examiners assume that candidates already have a working knowledge of the TL script.

Most MFL course materials do now feature handwritten texts. Russian manuals begin with the individual letters of the Cyrillic alphabet, both printed and cursive. Students not only learn how to read Russian script at character, word and sentence level. They are also encouraged to use it when writing Russian by hand. French, German, Italian and Spanish textbooks typically dispense with individual cursive character recognition practice. Although students are expected to understand handwritten messages, they are not encouraged to use the authentic foreign script when writing the TL by hand. Conventional wisdom apparently argues that Russian script, which is based on the unfamiliar Cyrillic alphabet, must be explicitly taught, while West European scripts, which are based on the familiar Roman alphabet, can be implicitly caught.

School handwriting policies

German federalism and French centralism extend to primary school handwriting policy-making within these respective countries. Germany's *Grundschulen* have a choice of three official cursive scripts (Stadt Mannheim 1998):

- *Lateinische Ausgangsschrift*, which Baden-Württemberg adopted in 1953
- *Schulausgangsschrift*, which the then GDR introduced in 1968
- *Vereinfachte Ausgangsschrift*, which various *Länder* have trialled since 1973

France's *instituteurs* teach one national style of cursive handwriting that has stood the test of time. *Du graphisme à l'écriture*, a document showing the correct strokes to be used when forming and joining letters in French handwriting, can be downloaded from the World Wide Web (Bonnet 1996).

Thomas, a Kent infant school teacher, has compared approaches to the teaching of handwriting in England and France. Her main findings (Thomas 1998) are worth summarising:

- the teaching of handwriting is a high priority in French infant and junior schools;
- French teachers and education professionals display a higher degree of knowledge of the principles underlying the teaching of handwriting;
- in France, joined handwriting is viewed as the facilitator to creative written expression whereas in England, teaching handwriting and creative expression are seen as quite separate;
- French teachers believe Art and PE are closely linked to the teaching of handwriting;
- there is a wide range of literature available to teachers in France that supports their understanding and development of their teaching of handwriting;
- the synergy between higher education institutes and local education authorities aids the teaching of handwriting as a high priority in initial teacher training and in continuing professional development.

Computers and handwriting

Normal writing instruments now share the educational stage with ICT. In both cases, the human factor – mental and manual dexterity and co-ordination – is paramount. While hand-printed lettering and hunt-and-peck typing may suffice for the interim, fluency and accuracy come with the skills of joined-up handwriting and touch-typing.

Both penmanship and keyboarding have advantages and limitations. Although pens and pencils are cheap, plentiful and portable, physical and mental co-ordination determines whether they generate calligraphy or cacography. ICT holds out a prospect of clear typography and better layouts for even untidy or dyspraxic students, but means dearer, scarcer and bulkier hardware too.

Penmanship and keyboarding are also complementary. Secretaries practise keying in from handwritten draft because the latter is the commonest form of draft in the workplace (Spencer 1999). Conversely, busy primary and SEN teachers may produce handwriting worksheets using dedicated software, e.g. *Handwriting for Windows* (Inclusive Technology 1999), to build and reinforce letter formation and joining skills. They may even encourage slower learners to use a word processing package enhanced with cursive fonts when preparing and submitting assignments that are meant to be handwritten (Bonnet 1996).

The educational benefits of electronic handwriting font technologies have been recognised by teachers of more advanced students too. Becker, a University of Wisconsin-Madison Germanist, has designed a *Sütterlin* computer font to solve the vexed problem of deciphering immigrant German family documents in the historical script (Becker 1995; Hoecherl-Alden & Köhler-Busch 1998). He has also found his computer-generated script to be an effective training model for archivists because the typeface is completely free of the stylistic idiosyncrasies that characterise many German-American manuscripts.

The technology of Natural Handwriting Recognition (NHR) empowers computers to decipher handwriting with greater speed and accuracy than human readers can muster. Among its pioneers were Soviet scientists with an educational mission in the late 1960s to evaluate Russian school students' cursive handwriting (Landwehr 1999). The world focus of NHR has long since shifted to business applications, particularly postal address, cheque, form, medical record and insurance claim automation. Unlike Optical Character Recognition (OCR), which handles machine-printed characters, and Intelligent Character Recognition (ICR), which processes separate characters hand-printed in boxes, NHR deploys complex image analysis algorithms to identify each character. It then recombines the letters and runs dictionary checks on the letter sequences to produce meaningful output (Rawson n.d.).

If computers can process printed letters more easily than handwritten characters, then the same is likely to hold true of human readers. The following study attempts to explore this hypothesis, with particular reference to foreign handwriting recognition difficulties of lower secondary school learners of French.

The study

In this section I turn to the action research itself. I describe:

- the geographical and institutional context of the study, with special reference to the high incidence of SEN in my school population;
- the design of the study and more particularly the definition of the TL handwriting recognition problem and the appropriateness of an ICT solution;
- the methods employed in the study, namely the sampling of learners as subjects, the nature of students' assignments and the monitoring procedures combining classroom observation and task error analysis.

I work in the Metropolitan Borough of South Tyneside in the North East of England. South Shields, in the east of the borough, is a pleasant seaside resort, burdened with more than its fair share of social, economic and educational disadvantage. A third of the 1,200 students in my over-subscribed 11–16 comprehensive school, now a DfEE-designated Technology College, qualify for free school meals. Typically 30% of the boys and 20% of the girls leave primary education with reading ages two or more years below their chronological ages. Although a tiny minority of these learners later transfer to local special schools, most remain in mainstream education receiving their full National Curriculum entitlement, including MFL.

At Harton School I have acquired a number of responsibilities over recent years in MFL and SEN impinging on the conduct of this study. I teach several Year 7 French and Year 8 German beginners' classes, averaging 25 students apiece. I monitor the progress of over 35 Year 7 students registered as having SEN, withdrawing individuals for basic skills practice, managing a paired reading scheme, collating literacy and numeracy learning targets and compiling Individual Education Plans. I offer in-class learning support in Year 7 Design Technology, English, French, Geography, History, ICT, Mathematics, Religious Education and Science. I word process the school's programmes, newsletters, annual reports and staff handbook. I also spend one lunch-hour a week at Oakleigh Gardens, a special school for students with profound and multiple difficulties, where I assist with ICT.

I had two goals in mind when I planned my investigation. First, identify the learning needs of students experiencing MFL pre-reading problems. Secondly, support the students as they negotiated solutions to such problems. While supporting learners in the classroom, I had come across students who could not decipher their own teachers' English styles of handwriting with speed and accuracy. Copying handwriting from the board is widely recognised by SEN professionals as a major challenge to students with literacy difficulties (McColl 2000). I surmised that transcribing authentic handwritten French would raise a further barrier in their case.

There remained the question of what help the students might require to confront and overcome this obstacle in their path. They could certainly familiarise themselves with TL handwriting by working with authentic handwritten letters and messages, but the school had neither a steady supply of suitable texts nor a French Assistant whose penmanship could be deployed to fill the gap.

Fortunately, an ICT solution to the problem presented itself. I chanced upon a source of authentic French script fonts on the World Wide Web (Verchery, Beaumale & Tassel n.d.). These fonts were developed to support the teaching of handwriting in France. Their designers were French primary school teachers who generously placed the fruits of their labours in the public domain as freeware. I have described elsewhere how to download and install these TrueType fonts (Wilson, 1999).

The next step was to gauge the calibre of the simulated script and to devise accessible, authentic and appropriate tasks. Two French primary school handwriting manuals (Zacharia 1996; Lacroix 1998) came to the rescue. In certain fonts, the simulation of individual handwritten characters proved to be impressively accurate, although the ligatures between letters were a little variable. Figure 3.1 shows how Times New Roman and PlumBAL, a pen-simulation font, transcribe the French equivalent of the English-speaking touch-typist's drill *the quick brown fox jumps over the lazy dog.*

Portez un vieux whisky à ce juge blond qui fume

Portez un vieux whisky à ce juge blond qui fume

Figure 3.1: French pangram transcribed in serif and cursive fonts

The primers also furnished sets of graded exercises to build up word and sentence handwriting skills, beginning with lower-case characters and progressing through punctuation marks to accented and capital letters. I planned to compile a similar hierarchy of tasks in my study to ensure progression and to challenge the high flyers who were likely to read TL handwriting with relative ease.

The participants in the study were all Year 7 beginners in French, who attended their twice-weekly one-hour MFL lessons in regular form registration groups. Each class of roughly twenty-five spanned a full range of ability, from high flyers to low achievers scoring reading ages of under seven years on the Suffolk Reading Scale. Students whose reading ages fall significantly below nine years tend to experience difficulties when they engage with the secondary school curriculum.

I taught some of these French classes alone, otherwise I delivered the lesson while a fellow linguist provided learning support. In the former instance, I integrated ICT into my course wherever it seemed appropriate to the topic or the learners in question. In the latter team-teaching case, one fortnightly sixty-minute period was regularly scheduled for MFL/ICT throughout the year.

At Harton School, the whole Year 7 intake receives one weekly 60-minute period of ICT, which is usually delivered by their English teachers. I give in-class support in many of these lessons, where the students learn the fundamentals of word processing with Word 2 or 97.

In the first MFL/ICT session, I build on this prior knowledge with several teaching objectives in mind:

- introduce and generate TL-specific characters beyond the basic Roman alphabet, e.g. à, ç, é, ï, ô, ù;
- raise awareness of, and sensitivity to, orthographic similarities and differences between English and the TL;
- develop keyboarding fluency and proof-reading accuracy when transferring TL copy-writing skills to the computer;
- provide an authentic, accessible and appropriate workplace task where both MFL and ICT skills are required and exploited.

I begin with the generation of accented characters via the Alt key. This foreign character entry method proved popular in an on-line survey which I conducted on the language teachers' forum Lingu@Net and whose findings were summarised on the World Wide Web[1]. The next step is the keying-in of French printed words, then sentences, using graded exercises modelled on a German bilingual secretaries' word processing manual (Koch n.d.).

The subsequent MFL/ICT session, where emphasis shifts from printed to handwritten draft, is also designed to serve a number of purposes:

- reinforce and develop existing MFL and ICT knowledge and skills;
- implement step-by-step progression from basic to more challenging authentic MFL/ICT tasks;
- promote decoding strategies when engaging with TL cursive handwriting.

The worksheet accompanying this unit about keying-in from handwritten French draft starts with a printout of the alphanumeric characters in French script and is here reproduced in Figure 3.2. I used MS Word for Windows with *CrayonL*, a pencil-simulating handwriting font, because this style was adopted in both French handwriting primers to which I had access.

Aa	Bb	Cc	Dd	Ee	Ff	Gg
Hh	Ii	Jj	Kk	Ll	Mm	Nn
Oo	Pp	Qq	Rr	Ss	Tt	Uu
Vv	Ww	Xx	Yy	Zz	Àà	Ââ
Çç	Èè	Éé	Êê	Ëë	Îî	Ïï
Œœ	Ôô	Ùù	Ûû	1	2	3
4	5	6	7	8	9	0

Figure 3.2: Alphanumeric characters in cursive font

I directed my Year 7 groups to keep this point of reference under constant review while they attempted the keyboarding exercises. On the reverse of the worksheet was a lower-case French pangram – a sentence where all the letters of the alphabet are represented – printed in the same pencil font. The students were asked to key this handwritten draft into Word using its standard Times New Roman serif font.

The follow-up exercises gradually introduced handwritten texts with pen-simulating fonts, longer sentences, punctuation marks, accented characters and capital letters, emulating the learning steps in the French primary school handwriting manuals.

I wanted my study to take account of both the process and the product of keying-in from handwritten draft. So classroom observation of the keyboarders as well as error analysis of their printouts contributed to data collection.

The outcomes

In this section, I present:

- the results of my classroom observations and task error analysis, showing the extent to which TL handwriting recognition challenged all MFL students and particularly those with learning difficulties;
- my conclusions arising from the study and recommendations for further research and development on integrating TL handwriting recognition into MFL teaching;
- a postscript listing what has happened locally within my school and nationally in the new MFL schemes of work in the TL handwriting recognition field since the completion of my project.

As predicted, many students found keying-in from handwritten French draft to be a challenging activity. Their experience of difficulty manifested itself not only in their printouts but also in their verbal reactions while attempting the tasks in the ICT room.

The roles of dispassionate researcher and sympathetic teacher inevitably proved very hard to juggle. On the one hand, I wanted my students to consult one independent reference source – a printout of the alphanumeric characters in French script – as they decoded the draft, so the results would not be skewed by my intervention. On the other hand, I was reluctant to leave individuals floundering or disaffected.

The students with special educational needs showed little hesitation to voice their concerns. During one session, a boy with behaviour difficulties protested about my non-intervention: *'But sir, you're a special needs teacher, you're supposed to help!'* In another lesson, a group of low achievers even persuaded my support teacher to hand-print the text of the pangram, which they claimed was an illegible scrawl.

Even the better performers found the mixture of thick and thin character strokes of the pen-simulating font quite disconcerting. They also asked me for reassurance as they strove to make sense of each word as well as its constituent letters. Only a few very able students took the tasks in their stride.

On the positive side, when questioned, most students conceded the relative elegance of the French national handwriting style. They also acknowledged the authenticity of the keyboarding tasks they were invited to complete. The slower learners preferred ICT to penmanship, one of them remarking that the former *'doesn't ache'* his hand.

Analysis of the printouts revealed wide quantitative and qualitative variations in the students' responses to the tasks. Although the high flyers generally reproduced the texts with speed and accuracy, the slow learners only managed to complete the first task requiring a single sentence pangram to be keyed in.

Almost two-thirds of the 26 letters of the alphabet represented in this pangram generated misspellings. One of the sixteen – w – was transcribed in no less than eight different wrong ways. The problematic four vowels a, e, o, u and twelve consonants b, f, h, k, l, n, r, s, v, w, x, z are reproduced in French script in Figure 3.3 with their miscues printed in brackets.

a	[i] [e]	h	[f] [r]	o	[a] [e]	v	[n] [r] [u]
b	[l]	k	[b] [f] [r]	r	[n] [s]	w	[m] [n] [nu] [r] [ru] [rv] [u] [v]
e	[a] [i] [u]	l	[b] [f]	s	[a] [l]	x	[sc] [se]
f	[l]	n	[m] [r]	u	[e] [ii] [ll] [y]	z	[3]

Figure 3.3: Transcription error analysis

If so many of the lowercase characters in the French script lent themselves to such confusion, then their uppercase equivalents were liable to prove even more vexatious. Fortunately, uppercase characters are confined in French handwriting to initial letters of proper nouns and sentence-opening words. Uppercase titles, signs, acronyms and the like are printed in block capitals.

Conclusions and recommendations

Beyond peradventure, authentic handwritten French is a challenge to students with learning difficulties.

Even confident and competent readers need reassurance when engaging with TL handwritten draft.

Most students appreciate the authenticity of handwriting-to-print tasks as prescribed in the French keyboarding unit.

French handwriting recognition requires far more practice, and differentiated activities, than was feasible in the present study.

Using one of the authentic handwriting fonts, MFL teachers might word process signs and flashcards with key vocabulary and phraseology for display in non-ICT lessons to ensure skills transfer.

MFL teachers might consider putting one or several of the fonts at the disposal of their students as an active learning model or an authentic keyboarding resource for MFL correspondence.

Further research is required to determine whether students' bottom-up cursive letter recognition skills would benefit from explicit teaching of individual cursive letter formation, perhaps via nonsense words.

Postscript

When CrayonL was later installed on the school's network, Year 7 students began integrating it into their MFL/ICT work without further prompting. The pencil font appeared in signatures on French greetings cards and in the caption of the tourist poster in Figure 3.4. CrayonL even became the quite unselfconscious font of choice of several Year 9 SEN students while word processing reviews of the film *Titanic* for their English teacher.

Figure 3.4: Example of new cursive font application

The new Key Stage 3 schemes of work encourage students to engage with French cursive script from the outset (DfEE, 2000):

> *Displays of letters should use French handwriting in order to familiarise pupils with authentic French handwriting at an early stage in their learning.* (Unit 2: En famille)
>
> *(Pupils) compare French and English handwriting and note the letters and numbers which are formed differently and are likely to cause a problem to an English reader.* (Unit 6: Comment tu t'amuses?)

Although neither unit mentions computer-generated French handwriting, this font technology has enormous potential as an alternative learning model and source of authentic materials. The best ICT resources appeal to the curiosity, imagination and ingenuity of teachers and students alike. They also represent authentic and accessible solutions to real human needs. Their appropriateness lies in the sense of ownership that they confer upon their users.

Acknowledgement

I wish to thank my brother Dr Tom Wilson, an independent medical informatics consultant in Minneapolis, for his valuable comments, advice and encouragement when he reviewed the manuscript of this chapter.

Bibliography

Becker D A, 'Silicon Sütterlin.' in *Die Unterrichtspraxis,* Vol 28(1): 52–56 (1995)

Bonnet J, *Du graphisme à l'écriture.* MS Word document in downloadable file www.ac-aix-marseille.fr/bleue/element/graphisme/GRAPHISM.ZIP (1996)

DfEE, *Schemes of Work. KS3: Modern foreign languages – French.* MS Word documents in downloadable file www.standards.dfee.gov.uk/local/secondary/docs/mfl2fr.zip (2000)

DfEE and QCA, *Modern foreign languages.* London: Department for Education and Employment & Qualifications and Curriculum Authority (1999)

Hoecherl-Alden G and M Köhler-Busch, 'Expanding on authenticity: a case for immigrant letters, photographs, and other German-Americana in the language classroom.' in *Die Unterrichtspraxis,* Vol 31(1): 38–46 (1998)

Inclusive Technology, *Handwriting for Windows Version 2.1.* www.inclusive.co.uk/catalog/handwrit.htm (1999)

Jameson M, *Dyslexia and modern foreign languages: strategies for success.* Presentation given at the First International Multilingualism and Dyslexia Conference, Manchester, 17–19 June (1999)

Koch, *Fremdsprachliche Textverarbeitung: Englisch. Französisch.* (Rinteln: Merkur Verlag (n.d.))

Lacroix B, *6e. Cahier d'écriture.* (Paris: Bordas, 1998)

Landwehr R, *Teaching computers to read* www.bizjournals.com/denver/stories/1999/02/01/smallb1.html (1999)

McColl H, *Modern languages for all.* (David Fulton, 2000)

Rawson C E, *Breaking down the last document automation barriers.* www.infotivity.com/hwr.htm (n.d.)

Spencer S, *Learn to keyboard.* (Heinemann, 1999)

Stadt Mannheim, *Schulen und Bildungswege in Mannheim.* www.mannheim.de/internetrathaus/schulver/faecher.html (1998)

Thomas F, 'Une question de writing: a comparative study' in *Support for learning,* Vol 13(1): 43–45 (1998)

Verchery C, C Beaumale and P Tassel, *Polices d'écriture cursive.* Freeware TrueType fonts downloadable from http://services.worldnet.net/logedu/cursive.htm (n.d.)

Wilson D R, *Applying ICT appropriately to MFL. Web skills: Files.* www.tomwilson.com/david/case/files.html (1999)

Zacharia M, *6–8 ans. Mon deuxième cahier d'écriture.* (Paris: Retz, 1996)

Notes

1 http://bris.ac.uk/education/ml/accents.htm

Chapter 4

Interactive oral work at a distance

Sue Hewer and Lesley Shield

The missing component in virtual learning environments (VLEs)

There is no doubt that web-based teaching and learning environments provide an exciting prospect for those involved in distance education. However, for the linguist, there is a missing component in most VLEs available to date, namely that of enabling students to engage in real time interactive oral work. With the advent of a number of websites which offer voice chat, the facility to hold on-line spoken discussions seems to be within grasp. However, in the experience of the Centre for Modern Languages at the Open University (OU), such a facility is more likely to bring about real and lasting language learning gains if it is situated within a VLE designed to meet the needs of language learners and their tutors, and over which the institution has control. The Centre for Modern Languages at the Open University has undertaken a number of studies into various on-line language learning media since 1995 and brought experiences from those studies to the on-going design of an OU in-house VLE, known as *Lyceum*. Evaluative studies of its use with volunteer students at differing levels and studying either French or German were undertaken in 1999–2000 in order to establish its potential roles in distance language learning. These studies focused on task design, the role of the tutor and the role of the student, in all cases taking into account the needs of the students within the overall course context and characteristics of the media used. This chapter draws on the papers of the various studies, some of which were internal documents and others which have been published. A list of the papers concerned is contained in the bibliography at the end of the chapter.

Meeting the need with telephone tutorials

The Centre for Modern Languages has been conscious of the need to provide oral interaction for all students since the first language course was launched in 1995 (L120 : French : post-GCSE/Standard Grade). Two initial problems arose with regard to attendance at face-to-face tutorials. Firstly, for students living in remote areas of Britain and for students scattered across mainland Europe, the distance to the nearest OU centre was too great. Secondly, a number of students were unable to attend due to their personal, family or employment circumstances. It was decided to try to meet the needs of these students by replacing face-to-face tutorials with telephone tutorials which were monitored and evaluated within a project which became known as the Telephone Tutorials Monitoring project. Tutorial groups comprised some eight students and a tutor.

The tutors concerned received some generic training but, in the first year of the project, did not receive any subject-specific training. They set up the kind of activities that they would have done in face-to-face mode, which, it was assumed, would focus on the development of oral fluency, since this is the most difficult aspect of language use to develop when studying alone and difficult to deal with in one-way media such as print, audio and video tapes. It was further assumed that students would be encouraged to develop the use of the kind of linguistic functions required in discussion, such as creating opportunities to intervene, to establish and defend one's own standpoint, and to question the standpoints of others. The assumptions were ill-founded for two reasons which it is important for distance educators to take into account.

Firstly, there was a discrepancy in the views about the purpose of face-to-face tutorials between some of the course tutors and their managers. The assumption that the focus would be on the development of oral fluency was proved to be false in that, for example, some of the activities provided for students were oral gap fills which could have been done equally well on paper. While much has been written about the student working at a distance, less has been written about tutors working at a similar distance from their students and from each other. When distance learning tutors work in the institutional base, both formal and informal communication can occur with ease. However, there is an increasing tendency for on-line tutors to work at a distance from the host institution thereby making on-going monitoring of content and delivery difficult. This begs questions about the potential variability of the students' learning experiences. There is no doubt that such variability occurs in campus-based courses. However, it is more easily detected and rectified under these circumstances than where a course leader might never come into contact with students, and only meet tutors in large meetings on one or two occasions during the academic year.

The characteristics of the medium

The provision of telephone tutorials was a rapid response to need. The assumption was made that it would be possible to deliver tutorials by telephone conference comparable to those delivered in face-to-face mode. Account had not been taken of the characteristics of the medium of telephone conferencing and the effect that they would have on the delivery of the tutorials. Firstly, the lack of visual clues meant the loss of body language, which made it difficult for students to anticipate when another student was coming to the end of what they had to say. This resulted in the tutor feeling it necessary to manage turn taking, thereby minimising the opportunities available to students to practise the linguistic functions associated with taking part in discussions. The need for managed turn taking was further exacerbated by a second characteristic of telephone conferencing. When ordinary telephones are used, it is not possible in a conference call for anyone to intervene in a conversation until a silence occurs. To predict the end of an utterance and to have the right words ready at the start of the silence are skills which this level of learner found difficult to exercise. A third characteristic of the medium, the inability to display text or images, resulted in an excessive degree of preparation by students during the first year of the project. Tutors were obliged to send out in advance the tutorial plan and any texts or images associated with the activities. In order to build up the confidence of students, the nature of the activities was also usually included. For example, students might be sent two apparently similar but slightly different pictures and be asked to be ready to identify the differences. This resulted in students reading from prepared scripts which replicated the kind of oral activities which they undertook alone when they were required to make recordings to send to their tutor for assessment. In the second year of the course, tutors were provided with strategies to overcome some of the difficulties imposed by the medium, for example, sending out texts or pictures with encouragement to the students to gather together certain vocabulary and structures, without being told what the actual nature of the related activity was. The application of the strategies resulted in more spontaneous speech in the second year of the project, but the conclusion was reached that replication of a face-to-face tutorial format within another medium did not enable students to achieve comparable learning outcomes. It was felt that a change of approach was necessary involving a focus on the development of spontaneous speech, with the tutor acting as facilitator, and students taking more responsibility for their own learning. It was decided to move to a task-based approach and to introduce the use of e-mail in addition to telephone conferences.

Telephone conferences and e-mail

The investigation into the combined use of e-mail and telephone conferencing took place in 1997 with the first phase of the *OnLine Language Learning project* (OL3-1). The change from a tutorial framework to that of a task-based one was influenced by the findings of Chun (1994) that the use of topic-related text chat in advance of oral activity improved performance in the oral activity. In the case of the Centre for Modern Languages, it was decided to set up tasks lasting from between two and four weeks which consisted of a kick-off and round-up telephone conference and e-mail activity during the intervening weeks. Both French and German students were involved, drawn from courses at all three levels then in presentation. The addition of e-mail to telephone conferencing created a hybrid VLE offering both asynchronous and synchronous communication media. It was hoped asynchronous e-mail would promote rehearsal of appropriate vocabulary, structures and functions and would encourage reflective learning while the synchronous telephone conferences would foster comparatively spontaneous language production.

Typically students would receive an indication of the nature of the task and the kinds of roles involved in e-mail, along with the e-mail addresses of all the members of the group in advance of the first telephone conference. During the conference, they would get to know the other members of the group, find out more about the task from their tutor, be allocated a role within the task, and identify the members of their sub-group. There would then be some two weeks of e-mail activity during which the sub-groups collaborated to complete their sub-task. At the end of the e-mail activity, there would be a final telephone conference which took the form of competitive presentations and questions, or a debate. In most cases, the tutor was also allocated a role which they played during the final telephone conference.

The model adopted for the design of the task, and tasks set up in subsequent studies, was one of collaboration and conflict in order to give students a real purpose for reading, writing, listening and speaking in the target language. For example, a group of Level 1 German learners were divided into three sub-groups, each of which represented one of the plants owned by a pan-European company preparing to receive some important visitors from Japan. The job of the sub-groups was to put forward a case for their plant hosting the visit. In between the first and last telephone conference the sub-groups worked together to build up and set out their case. During the final telephone conference, they each put forward their case and took questions from members of the other two groups and the tutor, while the tutor played the role of decision maker at head office. The tasks were entirely course-related and took place during the normal running of the course.

Evidence

Recordings of the final telephone conferences of OL3-1 provided evidence of a higher incidence of student talk than was apparent during the previous telephone tutorials despite the continuing lack of visual clues, of greater risk taking by students and of longer and more complex utterances, probably resulting from the rehearsal of structures and vocabulary during the e-mail phase. It was concluded that the generic model adopted for the tasks was appropriate, that the shift of role of the tutor resulted in greater student involvement with the task and the kind of language required for its completion and that students exercised their existing life skills and became more actively engaged with the extended task than they had been with the short exercises which made up the telephone tutorials. The most significant lack in provision identified by students was the lack of feedback about errors. In later studies, some tutors sent out e-mails to the full group identifying and explaining errors without attributing them. Where text chat has been available, individual errors leading to a breakdown in communication have been dealt with via private messages. Where tutors have been allocated a role within a task, they have been able to ask for repetition or clarification without dropping out of their role when they have felt that other students were losing the meaning of what was being said.

Conclusions

Analysis of data collected during the course of the OL3-1 research gave rise to the hypothesis (Stevens & Hewer 1998) that performance in the foreign language improves when learners can:

- collaborate with each other between scheduled events;
- engage in meaningful exchanges;
- receive instant feedback from their peers via a synchronous medium such as the telephone.

Internet telephony

In 1998 the OU began to work experimentally with an Internet-based audio conferencing tool called *VoxChat*. Given the centrality of oral communication in OU courses and the findings arising from the previous experimentation of the Centre for Modern Languages with the use of telephone conferencing, staff at the Centre were given the opportunity to use *VoxChat* + e-mail + website in the FLUENT project and *VoxChat* + e-mail + a shareware package called *Rendezvous* within the second phase of the OnLine Language Learning project (OL3-2). The core tool in both projects was *VoxChat* which provided significant advantages over telephone conferencing and opened up new possibilities for the task designer, new challenges for the tutor and new opportunities for the learner.

VoxChat offered a number of advantages over telephone conferencing which are of interest in themselves and which also serve to point out the need to identify the characteristics of a medium and the kind of learning that it is capable of delivering when considering its use in language teaching and learning.

On logging into *VoxChat*, the student goes to the room allocated to the group by clicking on the appropriate name in the list provided. Once there, the student finds a list of the names of the people already present, to which their own name has been added. Once in the room, students can talk by either holding down the talk button via the left-hand mouse button, or by holding down the space bar. Permanent breakout rooms can be created as can impermanent rooms as the need arises. While it was possible to set up a second telephone conference alongside the core conference, this had to be timetabled in advance and it was difficult for the tutor to migrate to the second conference once it had started. The ability to set up a number of different rooms, which can be visited by the tutor at any time, encourages the design of highly interactive tasks based on the information gap model. Tutors found the management of sub-groups in breakout rooms challenging, not least in knowing when and how to intervene and when to leave well alone. In some instances, students stopped talking when the tutor dropped in and waited for an intervention. In other instances, students simply carried on with their discussion and ignored the presence of the tutor. Interestingly, recordings of the sessions indicate that the target language was used almost exclusively in sub-group discussions when the tutor was not present. This was also the case during non-scheduled meetings set up by students which are discussed below. Recordings of individual sessions were made on the server, with the written permission of students, in order to enable researchers to pursue their own areas of interest such as the analysis of the discourse in terms of length and complexity of sentences, extent of tutor talk compared with student talk, and the styles of different tutors, taking into account the levels of the learners concerned.

In *VoxChat*, a microphone icon is displayed against the name of the person who is talking, thereby overcoming one of the drawbacks of telephone conferencing when you do not know your fellow students well enough to identify them by voice. As indicated above, there were very few instances of students interrupting during the telephone tutorials, because of the need to wait for a silence. *VoxChat* works in full duplex mode which means that interruptions can be made at any time since up to six speakers can be heard at any one time. Students soon found that if they kept pressing the Speak button, the microphone icon by their name flickered, indicating to others their desire to speak. These two facilities seemed to improve students' self-confidence and willingness to speak. They provided an important part of the context within which they were working, which was absent from the telephone tutorials. They also enabled students to work within protocols more closely related to those of face-to-face discussion than was possible with the phone.

VoxChat has a text chat facility which was not exploited as such within tasks. However, as indicated above, it proved useful in enabling tutors to send a private text message to a student experiencing communication difficulties without having to interrupt the flow of the discussion in which that student was participating. This is an important facility through which to provide immediate and individual feedback. Some students found an alternative and, to some extent, surprising use for text chat in that they used it to talk amongst themselves while the tutor was talking, sometimes passing comments about what was going on, sometimes talking about entirely extraneous matters. Since text chat is not a mainstream communications medium, and since its use alongside an oral medium involves the student in switching between oral and written production, it is debatable whether or not it has a useful role to play within tasks designed to enable students to cope with real world situations in the target language. This debate continues within the Centre for Modern Languages.

Unlike telephone conferences which have to be set up in advance and moderated by an operator, the *VoxChat* server at the OU was up and running 24 hours a day, seven days a week. Students were thus able to meet when they wanted to, without a tutor, and to complement their use of asynchronous e-mail by synchronous oral interaction. This facility was much appreciated and much used by students, some of whom continue to meet long after the completion of the pilot study. Again, recordings show that the bulk of the talk was in the target language. The ability to meet to talk, at local call rate, enabled students to move from written to spoken rehearsal and appeared to contribute to the improved quality of their oral performance during the final phase of the task. There were no instances of people backing away from participating in these sessions and students tended to show a marked lack of dependence on the tutor in their sub-group work.

Audio-graphics: VoxChat + e-mail + Rendezvous

The OL3-2 project was designed to investigate the potential of audio-graphics taking into account the use made of pictures and texts by the tutors during the Telephone Tuition project. A shareware product called *Rendezvous* was used alongside *VoxChat* and e-mail. *Rendezvous* enables tutors and students to place an image or text document onto a whiteboard which when sent is then transmitted almost instantly to all group members logged on and in the group's room. It is also possible to send files to other group members which, at the time of the pilot study, were transferred very rapidly. In addition, there is a text chat facility similar to the one available in *VoxChat*. The whiteboard is mono-dimensional which meant that it was not possible to put up a background, on which the students could create and edit a foreground without destroying the initial image. However, despite these shortcomings, the whiteboard was used to good effect to display a plan of a proposed new town based on an existing village on to which villagers and planners indicated their intended locations for areas such as an industrial estate, shopping centre, housing complexes and leisure zones. It was also used simply to display pictures for discussion at the time of the scheduled meeting in activities such as guessing the purpose of an invention or creating story lines to go with a series of pictures. The ability to display images is very attractive to the task designer. They are important in focussing the attention of a student at the beginning of an activity and they can provide a reason for talking in the course of a task. The facility is also attractive to the tutor who can use it as a presentational tool, particularly with less experienced learners. Students appear to enjoy having something to look at other than the *VoxChat* screen, given that scheduled sessions tended to last between 45 and 60 minutes.

Feedback from the FLUENT and OL3-2 projects

Findings from the FLUENT project as described by Shield, Rodine, Hauck & Haezewindt (1999) indicate that most learners enjoyed this approach to learning and were very enthusiastic about the opportunity to interact verbally with other distance learners. Some learners voluntarily spent up to seven hours a week on-line in addition to the scheduled event. One wrote that this method of studying ...

> *... gave me the opportunity to talk to a group of people most of whom I had never met before, in a purposeful way. It was enjoyable.*

While another remarked:

> *I particularly enjoyed communicating with other people whom I have not ever met especially through the medium of German.*

Responses to post-activity questionnaires were enthusiastic, referring to *'feeling a team member'* – something which home-based distance learners may not experience very often during their studies – and the fact that each activity *'gave individuals and groups the opportunity to develop it as they wished and encouraged discussion before the session'*. Learner confidence also appears to have improved:

> *I have noticed an improvement in my oral German already and I have learned not to worry about making mistakes.*

Lyceum

While the OL3-2 project was running, work was being done by the Academic Computing Service in the OU on an integrated learning environment called *Lyceum* which incorporated *VoxChat*, but which also offered an interactive whiteboard and, ultimately, a concept mapper and screen grabber. The OU's *Lyceum* is in no way connected with the proposed Microsoft tool of the same name. The *VoxChat* component was much the same as that described above. However, the whiteboard was a great improvement on the one found in *Rendezvous* in that it had both a background and a foreground. This meant that, in OL3-3, it was possible to provide backgrounds on which students could place objects and remove and/or relocate them without rubbing out the background. This feature is particularly important for language learners because it creates reasons for offering explanations and provides visual clues to meaning. A whiteboard with both background and foreground can be saved by a single student within a sub-group and opened up again in a breakout room for sub-group work. The results of the sub-group work can then be taken back to the plenary room for sharing with the rest of the group by the same method. The small-scale pilot study of the use of *Lyceum* indicated that students enjoyed working within an integrated environment, experienced few problems in making full and independent use of the tools, and considered that the nature of the task, the supportive VLE and the consultant role played by the tutor provided a valuable learning experience.

Task types

As a result of the various projects undertaken by the Centre for Modern Languages during the last five years, it is felt that the kind of extended task described above is possibly the best use of *Lyceum* for adult distance learners, working at A level/Higher Grade and above, although consideration is currently being given to the development of a taxonomy of shorter task types suitable for sub-GCSE/Standard Grade learners. There is no doubt that a VLE which combines an interactive sound facility, graphics capable of being edited on-line and, in the future, on-line text editing and shared viewing of web pages has much to offer younger or less experienced learners provided that task designers and tutors understand the nature of the media to which they have access and their role in language teaching and learning and tutors/teachers can adapt to the changed role of facilitator and manager of learning, rather than knowledge source. It is to be hoped that suitably designed VLEs will be used not only to support adult distance learners, but to foster international links at all levels and to maintain the teaching of minority languages at all levels where class numbers do not justify the provision of a face-to-face teacher.

Bibliography

Chun D M, 'Using computer networking facilities to facilitate the acquisition of interactive competence' in *System,* Vol 22: No. 1 Pergammon (1994)

Hauck M, S Hewer and L Shield, Online media for language learning, *CILT CALL Report*, (CILT, 1999)

Hauck M and B Haezewindt, 'Adding a new perspective to distance (language) learning and teaching – the tutor's perspective' in *ReCALL,* 11 (2): 39–46, (1999)
On-line: www.cti.hull.ac.uk/eurocall/recall/r_online.htm

Hewer S, Facilitating interactive on-line tasks for distance language learners using interactive audio, text and graphics tools, paper given at EuroCall conference, 1999

Hewer S and L Shield, 'Building up fluency online' in *Netword* (CILT, 1999)

Hewer S, OL3-3 'Lyceum pilot study with L221 CML students: October–December 1999', *Internal CML/OU report* (2000)

Hewer S, M Kötter, C Rodine and L Shield, 'Criteria for the selection of online tools for fluency-orientated tasks for distance language learners' Paper given at CAL99

Kötter M, 'The FLUENT Report', *Internal CML/OU Report* (2000)

Kötter M, L Shield and A Stevens, 'Real-time audio and email for fluency: promoting distance language learners' oral and aural skills via the Internet' in *ReCALL,* 11 (2), pp.47–54, (1999) On-line: www.cti.hull.ac.uk/eurocall/recall/r_online.htm

Lamy M-N and L Shield, 'Deux téléconférences pour l'auto-apprentissage d'une langue étrangère: synchronie ou asynchronie?' *Paper given at the UNTELE conference* (2000)

Shield L, C Rodine, M Hauck and B Haezewindt, 'Supporting autonomous learners' *The FLUENT project:- creating richer on-line communities to support the distance language learner,* paper delivered at the COMned conference (1999)

Shield L, M Hauck and M Kötter, 'Talking to strangers: reflections on the use of voice over Internet for language learning purposes' [working title], for submission to *C@lling Japan*

Shield L, M Hauck and M Kötter, 'Taking the distance out of distance learning' *Proceedings of BALEAP 99,* (Leeds University Press: Leeds & Online 2000)

Shield L, M Hauck and S Hewer, 'Talking to strangers – the role of the tutor in developing target language speaking skills at a distance' paper presented at UNTELE 2000, *Compiègne, France*

Stevens A and S Hewer, 'From policy to practice and back', *Proceedings LEVERAGE conference,* Cambridge, 1998
On-line: http://greco.dit.upm.es/~leverage/conf1/hewer.htm

PART TWO

Case studies

The four chapters in this part are all contributed by practising teachers and each one is concerned with critical reflection on their experience of using ICT with their students. These studies make limited reference to the literature or to theoretical frameworks. However, the students themselves are given a major role in the evaluative process, especially in the chapters by Wright and Hagger-Vaughan. This device leads to interesting findings about the effectiveness of the learning activities and the role of technology. Involving students in the evaluation process is shown to contribute positively to their learning. These studies demonstrate that action research by teachers can have a valuable role to play in enhancing learning. Here are some useful examples of how to design action research and how to give the learner a voice in the process.

As in Part 1, the writers have adopted a range of technologies and adapted them to their specific contexts. Teachers have been doing this since education began. What is important about these studies is the critical reflection that the writers bring to bear upon the innovations that they have been involved in. Interestingly, in these studies, it is apparent that learners can be quite precise about the way in which learning is supported by a particular tool. The reader who is seeking practical tips on how to use ICT may not glean much from these studies. However, their value lies in showing how the technology can support learning and how learners can develop their strategies and skills – not so much how to use ICT but why.

Chapter 5

Pupils' reflections on the benefits of ICT as a tool to support their modern language learning

Lesley Hagger-Vaughan

Context

Shireland Language College is an 11–16 inner city Language College in the West Midlands. The College has 800 pupils and is situated in a linguistically and culturally diverse area. Almost 50% of pupils at the College receive free school meals and unemployment in the area is high, currently at around 24%. Students are able to study French, German, Panjabi, Urdu, Mandarin Chinese, Japanese and Spanish supported by state of the art technology. The revised National Curriculum clearly stresses that pupils should be given opportunities to apply and develop their ICT capability through the use of ICT tools to support their learning in all subjects. In addition, there has been a new emphasis on ICT in the revised Programme of Study for Modern Foreign Languages with five requirements which specify the use of ICT. On becoming a Language College in 1998, our first priority was to develop a facility which would enable all pupils to benefit from the regular use of ICT to support their modern language learning. The old staff room was transformed into a multimedia World Languages Centre which houses a twenty position *Tandberg* Educational Multimedia Learning Centre. Each student PC is fitted with a *Divace* digital recorder and connected back to the central teacher console with full monitoring and intercom facilities available to the teacher. In addition to the multimedia World Languages Centre, the pupils also have access to an interactive whiteboard for whole class teaching and presentations.

Research focus

Often research findings are based on statistics and teachers' views and perceptions. The aim of this action research project is to give voice to the students. As educators, it is essential that we take into account the views of students when taking decisions which affect their learning. Also, in this way, we have an opportunity to consider how best we can enable students to learn and to encourage them to become life-long learners of modern foreign languages with particular regard to the role that ICT has to play within this. Within the research project, we aimed to investigate the impact of a number of ICT applications on pupils' skills of listening, reading, speaking and writing in German.

The target group

The target group consisted of eighteen pupils from a middle ability Year 10 German Group working at Foundation GCSE level and studying Module 2 of the SEG Modular GCSE Course: Organising a Visit to a German Speaking Country. The group was chosen because of its challenging nature as it included a variety of pupils with particular learning needs. The group consisted of several disaffected boys who needed very carefully structured lessons with clear targets and lots of positive feedback to ensure that they did not underachieve. Also, in the group were a number of girls who were rather lacking in confidence and self-esteem, together with a number of pupils with erratic attendance. There were also several very keen and highly motivated students who worked well in any situation almost regardless of approach and resource. All pupils followed GNVQ Part 1 in either ICT or Business so most had basic ICT skills and a number of the group had PCs at home.

Planning and conducting the research

At the beginning of the research period pupils completed a questionnaire which asked them to identify their strengths and weaknesses in terms of skill areas and their preferred learning style. This was used as a basis for planning the Module 2 unit of work and the integration of ICT into this work plan. Pupils made a broader use of ICT than might normally be the case in this period of time in order to enable them to focus more clearly on the impact of a range of ICT applications and to make comparisons. ICT was used for presentation purposes for practice and for performance. Pupils were often given a choice as to the task and the order of tasks they should complete. They could also choose whether to work independently or with a partner.

The action research was carried out over a six-week period and during this time pupils kept an ICT log in which they recorded details of tasks, methods of working and the perceived progress made. At the end of the six-week period they completed an evaluation sheet and reflected on their overall progress.

Project analysis

INTERACTIVE WHITEBOARD

The interactive whiteboard was used to introduce new vocabulary and structures which pupils found to be a very exciting alternative to the traditional flash-card/OHP presentation because of the multimedia nature of the resource. Pupils can easily take the lead and enjoy the variety of tasks. The focus is very much on speaking and listening and pupils are encouraged to concentrate on correct pronunciation and intonation. There are also opportunities for reading and writing. In fact, the whiteboard is an excellent tool for the teaching of structure and grammar. Did the pupils agree?

> *It is good to hear a different voice in German to the teacher.*
>
> *I like it when we teach the lesson – there are lots of different activities – I like the one where you listen and choose the correct answer.*
>
> *You can involve the whole class together – it is very interactive so you can all enjoy it more.*
>
> *It is helpful for learning to pronounce new words and phrases.*

EXPRESSIONS[1]

Pupils worked on this multimedia software individually and in pairs to practise the situation *At the tourist office*. They had a self-help sheet prepared by the languages assistant and then worked through tasks at their own pace. They could choose listening, reading and speaking tasks and the translation facility enabled them to listen better for gist and to clarify meaning and it assisted them in using reference materials appropriately and effectively.

> *I found it helpful to be able to choose the activities – I did all of them and felt I understood the whole story much better.*
>
> *It helps you better if you make a mistake because only you can hear it and no one else can.*
>
> *I liked using the translation facility on* Expressions; *it helped me understand the text without having to keep looking it up in the dictionary.*

ESSENTIALS[2]

Pupils used the *Essentials* program to practise key language aspects including numbers, currency, dates and time. All these are key elements for SEG Module 2 and pupils practised and then tested themselves and recorded their scores. They attempted each test at least three times with a view to improving their scores. Some pupils immediately recorded their scores and showed a clear improvement. Others were observed trying to improve their scores before writing down the results! This program is an excellent tool for differentiation, enabling pupils to work at their own pace and to pinpoint the area which they wish to work on. The *Essentials* program also enabled them to improve their own pronunciation by listening, repeating and then recording. Although many students enjoyed working independently, others missed collaborating with their friends and some preferred a hands-on money task with the teacher.

> *I like being able to test myself and see if I can improve.*
>
> *I preferred the hands-on task with the money.*
>
> *It helps you to concentrate better on your own.*
>
> *It helps you to think on your own but you cannot use other people's ideas to help your own.*

Encarta 99[3]

In order to enhance their cultural awareness and put Module 2 *Planning a Visit to a German Speaking Country* into context, pupils were given the task to prepare a briefing sheet in English for a business manager travelling to a German speaking country. During this task pupils extended their ICT skills, many learning new techniques with which to refine their work and enhance quality and accuracy.

> *I learned a lot about Switzerland – and I learned how to cut and paste.*
>
> *I learned how to crop pictures.*
>
> *It did not help me because I have* Encarta *at home but I think I'm better at editing text – but I helped Laura and showed her how to use it.*

Divace system

Pupils used the *Divace* system to listen to a hotel booking on a pre-recorded sound file and take down details. The pupils were able to work on the booking task at their own speed and during the task I intervened to pick out key vocabulary that was causing problems. They also took part in a hotel role play and used the system to work individually and in pairs. While they were involved in this task, I monitored their pronunciation and gave feedback where appropriate. This proved to be an efficient way of assessing oral skills and created a less daunting environment, leading to improved confidence.

> *It helps me because you do not get nervous to speak in front of the whole class.*
>
> *I like recording myself – if I make a mistake no one can hear apart from the teacher if she has tuned in.*
>
> *It helped me but if I went to Germany to book in a hotel I would get stuck.*

Research findings and conclusions

- *Which ICT Application have you found to be most helpful in your language learning and why?*

There was a very varied response from the group, which did not always relate to the perceived strengths and weaknesses highlighted in the first questionnaire. Some students cited a particular application because they felt it had enabled them to improve a specific skill. Others gave more general responses relating to the mode of working and consequent feelings of success and confidence. Frequent references were made to feeling less nervous or greater confidence and many responses related to being able to work at their own pace. Two students referred to having gained ICT skills as well as language skills.

> Encarta *because you learn a lot about Germany and I learned how to crop pictures.*
>
> *I found working with* Encarta *good because you don't have to write out pages of stuff.*
>
> *The application that has helped me the most is* Essentials *– I have managed to gain top scores in all sections – I feel much more confident now.*
>
> Essentials *– it helps you to concentrate better on your own.*
>
> *The interactive whiteboard – I enjoyed taking the lesson – it helps me to remember new words and phrases better.*
>
> Expressions *– I found it helpful to be able to choose the activities – I did all of them and felt I understood the whole story much better.*

- *Which language skills have improved the most through using ICT skills? Listening, reading, writing or speaking?*

Again, the responses from the students were very varied but in general they seemed to feel that it was predominantly their listening and speaking skills that had improved most through the use of ICT. Many of these students have at Key

Stage 3 taken part in a great deal of performance. However, as they have grown older, they have become more inhibited with speaking activities and clearly welcome the opportunity for individual practice. Listening to a tape is one of the least popular tasks amongst language learners – many of my students cited this as a weakness at the beginning of the project. Working with the *Divace* system at their own pace and with private monitoring has improved their feeling of success. They have frequent opportunities to repeat and improve pronunciation and the *Essentials* software gives frequent feedback and tangible success which they can clearly see as their scores improve. The ICT tools maximise their exposure to the target language and help them to consolidate.

> *Listening because I can listen as often as I like and then I can understand.*
>
> *Speaking because I think I can speak more clearly when I am on my own.*
>
> *Listening as you can hear it over and over and at your own speed.*
>
> *My listening skills have improved the most.*

Most of the pupils did not take account of the considerable amount of reading that they have had access to in their ICT tasks – including reading directions on the interactive whiteboard, reading text on the *Expressions* CD-ROM or the reading skills associated with the fact-finding tasks. Reading was almost regarded as part and parcel of the task – which, considering that many of these pupils had cited reading as a skill which they find particularly difficult, underlines the immediate impact of non-paper based reading.

- *Have you learned any new ICT skills during your work?*

All but one student felt that their ICT skills had improved as well as their language learning skills. In terms of the National Curriculum requirements both for ICT and MFL pupils had been given *'the opportunity to apply and develop their ICT capability through the use of ICT tools to support their learning in MFL'*.

> *I am more confident about using foreign characters now.*
>
> *I have improved my presentation techniques and I have learned how to use* Encarta *for research.*
>
> *How to use* Encarta *and use the computer for recording speech.*
>
> *No not really – I have a computer at home which I use all the time.*

ICT is clearly a powerful teaching and learning tool, which allows for better differentiation. Many of the programs provide considerable support for those pupils who are not so confident and there are plenty of extension possibilities for more able pupils. Most significantly, ICT enables pupils to work more independently – a crucial aspect of language learning. They could work at their own pace and repeat tasks and listen to texts as often as they liked. Teacher-pupil interaction is very different – pupils are in greater control of their learning. The teacher is able to utilise the pupils' ICT skills in a different context. The teacher is able to work more intensely with groups of students when involved in working in the World Languages Centre and the interactive whiteboard offers a dynamic and exciting teaching environment when most pupils are on task.

In the last lesson of the project – Friday afternoon after a long Spring term – the pupils returned to the Languages Centre – I was feeling tired and jaded and fully expecting a less than enthusiastic response. The pupils came into the Centre, hung up their coats and just got on with one of the allocated tasks – one or two had a chat in the cloakroom and I held back from telling them to get on with it. Five minutes later the whole of the class were on task completely independently – I just sat back and watched them until one of the lads said: *'what are you doing, Miss?'* As always taking a risk is worth it, not only has my relationship with the group improved but their self-esteem has shot up, they feel special and they have really considered how they learn, what they have learned and how they learn best. In their view, their skills have improved and their confidence in their ability to succeed in languages has improved. To what extent they will achieve better in the Module 2 Examination is not yet clear but certainly, at the end of the six-week period, students felt successful and confident that at least one of their language skills had been considerably improved through the use of ICT.

Future strategies

This action research project has certainly informed our practice and in particular confirmed our belief that providing an ICT entitlement for our students within MFL is a crucial part of every student's language learning experience. As a department we need to continually review the role of the teacher within the modern languages classroom and to develop our work on learning styles to ensure that in our planning we cater for the very varied preferences and needs of our students.

At interviews, our Head teacher often asks candidates which resource they would bring into the school if money were no object. To my mind a multimedia learning centre, which allows pupils to improve all language learning skills and become independent learners is a must – every Modern Languages Department deserves one!

Notes

1 Software package produced by *Vektor*
2 Software package produced by *Vektor*
3 Microsoft encyclopedia on CD-ROM in most languages

Chapter 6

MOOtual MOOses: Shared creation rightfully wrought

Lesley Shield, Markus J. Weininger and Lawrence B. Davies

In this chapter, we present a case-study using MOO [Multi User Domain, Object Oriented] a text-based virtual learning environment [VLE] or *world of words* (only text is used to describe the VLE and its inhabitants, as well as for conversation). We describe the learning activity in which groups of EFL learners and their teachers were involved, evaluate its success and offer a series of guidelines for those wishing to use MOO with their own learners.

More than chat?

Many teachers bring learners to MOO to chat with other MOO-users. There is a learning curve associated with MOO which requires users to understand the interface and master a few basic commands. Once these skills have been acquired, however, MOO-users are able to do much more than talk with each other. Despite myths to the contrary, it is only necessary to know five MOO commands to operate successfully within such a VLE. Unlike standard chat rooms, of the sort supported by clients like Internet Relay Chat (see glossary), which permit users only to chat, MOO offers learners the opportunity to interact with the text-based environment that is MOO and with other live users, become part of a virtual community or even to extend the environment permanently. They can also interact with *bots*, MOO-based text-objects which imitate the behaviour and sometimes speech of real people or use in-MOO facilities such as libraries, on-line dictionaries or language games. To use MOO for chat alone, then, is to misunderstand its nature and to employ the wrong tool for the job.

We advocate a collaborative, constructivist approach to MOO, adopting and adapting Shneiderman's (1998) *relate-create-donate* approach for use with on-line learning activities. Shneiderman reports on learning experiences where computer science students work in collaborative groups (relate) to develop a project (create) that has outcomes which can be viewed or experienced by an audience beyond their immediate peer groups (donate). In this way, learners communicate with a wider audience and engage in a motivating and purposeful learning experience.

Beyond chat – activities to promote collaborative learning

In 1997, we designed a collaborative MOO and web-based project which aimed to bring together groups of learners of EFL and adult basic education students to work together in a virtual representation of Bamburgh on the North-East coast of England. Learners worked in collaborative teams to research any aspect of the virtual area they found interesting as a group (useful web page addresses or URLs were provided in MOO and on a supporting website). They would then produce and publish a web page via an easy-to-use web-editor, developed for the project. As we report (Shield & Weininger 1999), our first attempt at working with teachers and students from around the world in this way foundered for several reasons: technical, pedagogical, personal and practical. The second pilot study was more successful, although we found that learners either produced a web page or socialised with each other within the framework of developing a never-to-be-completed web page. Learners reported that they found the provision of the learning framework very useful, and were even motivated to continue meeting after the project had finished.

As a result, we designed a new project (the GrassRoots project). This was set up partly to investigate whether it would be possible to increase the number of participants without detrimentally affecting the outcomes, and partly to examine the effect of offering learners warm-up activities to acclimatise them to the MOO environment before participating in a main event.

Outcomes of the GrassRoots project

Five groups of learners took part in the GrassRoots project (Figure 6.1).

Origin	Age	Number	L1
Australia	16-42	10	English
Japan	18-22	30	Japanese
Korea	18-19	80	Korean
Sweden	15-16	30	Swedish
Ukraine	18-22	20	Ukrainian

Figure 6.1: Composition of GrassRoots project groups

The initial number of students involved in the GrassRoots project was approximately 130 from around the world. The project administrator, the teacher of the Japanese group, divided learners into groups of 5–6, group members coming from different countries. After the first three weeks of the project, he also organised regular on-line meetings between teachers. Learners and teachers were contacted via MOOmail (an in-MOO mailing system) and the project was explained to them. All instructions were also included on the supporting website. Learners were asked to go to the warm-up activities to acclimatise themselves to MOO and to get to know others in their group by using MOOmail, in-MOO bulletin boards and synchronous discussion about the topics for the warm-up activities. Although these activities had been very carefully planned to encourage learners to communicate with each other and to feed back on the warm-up activities, only the Australian learners did so. Some learners moved straight to the main event and, when they had described themselves appropriately (Figure 6.2a) began to build their own rooms (Figure 6.2b).

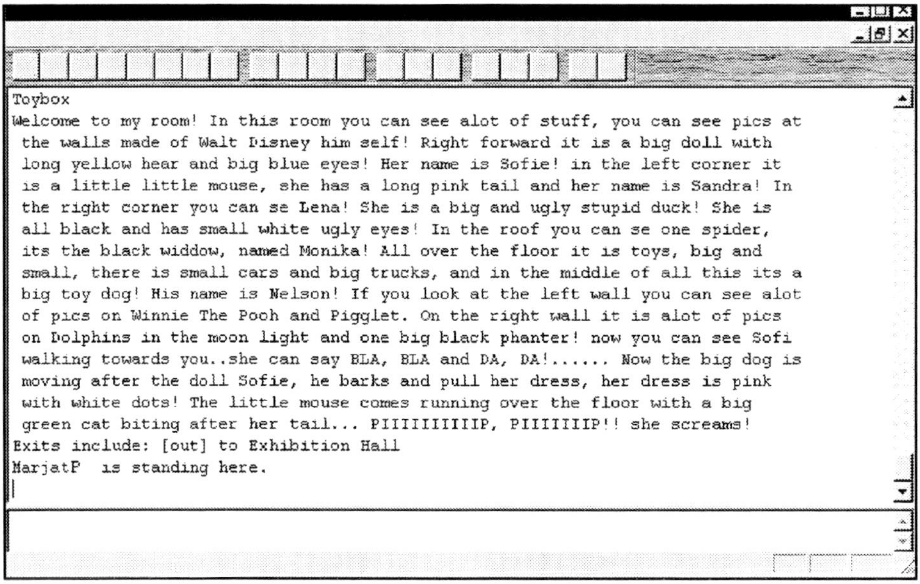

Figure 6.2a: MOO description and information file for 16-year-old Swedish learner

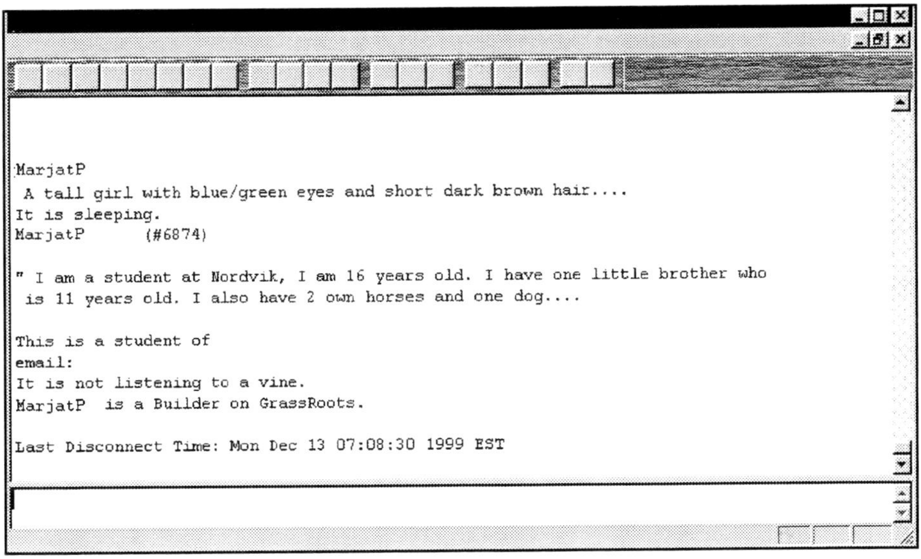

Figure 6.2b: Room description: 16-year-old Swedish learner

No group of learners managed to collaborate to develop a website during the three months available for the project. Interestingly, it was the younger learners (15–16 and the older adult basic education students) who were most motivated by the experience and who produced elaborate room descriptions. This may have been the result of their teachers' understanding of the underlying pedagogical tenets of collaboration, community and construction and their enthusiasm for the project.

Both teachers and learners did feed back their impressions of rooms to the builders, although teachers' evaluations were, unsurprisingly, more detailed than learners'.

From Len to MarjatP, Wednesday, 24th November 1999

```
Your room
Hi,
I really like your room idea. Your next step should be to begin
describing the room, show what we see when we LOOK at it. Remember that
we are now on the inside of the toybox.

You would type @DESC HERE AS and then whatever text you want us to see
when we LOOK at this room.
Get in touch with me when you're done with this, and we can look into
some more fun details that can be created. In this place we probably
should create some toys and it's actually possible to do that here at
GrassRoots. You could for instance create a wind-up duck that goes
'QUACK QUACK' and waddles around if you want --- or almost anything
else you can think up.

Len
```

Figure 6.3a: Teacher feedback to MarjatP (16)

From SallyC to Gemma, Monday, 13th December 1999
Hallo
you have a very differnet room, but it's nice!

Figure 6.3b: Swedish student's (16) evaluation of an Australian student's (42) room

Evaluating the experience

Although the GrassRoots Project did not fully reach its stated goals (learners progressing through warm-up activities to collaborative building and website design) because of time restrictions, it provided us with much valuable information about managing a project of this sort. Some students did, in fact, suggest working collaboratively with their partners (Figure 6.4), even if this did not come to complete fruition:

From Maria_f41 to Picachu, Wednesday, 24th November 1999
the garage
Hi,Picachu.I'm eager to add something to your garage.Would you mind?
Bye for now .Maria

Figure 6.4: Message from Swedish student (16) to Japanese student (19)

For students who provided evaluations of the project, it was, on the whole, a successful experience. There were, however, some drawbacks (Figure 6.5): Internet access (MOO is a 24-hour a day, 7-day a week technology which means learners with Internet access can log in at any time), telephone charges, time zone differences and more advanced MOO commands provided hurdles for some learners, while several were disappointed by their partners' non-response to their initial eager MOOmails introducing themselves.

The most particular aspect of Moo is that we can read our conversation, because Moo is a text-based society on internet. Visible conversation means that we can look over and analize what we talk. Of corse we write what we want to say, but Moo conversation is defferent from our writing, like a e-mail. It is closer to our real conversation. I think we can study a lot from it. Besides, we don't have to worry about out pronouciation. Moreover, we Japanese are said "very shy", but we can speak to foreigners easily in Moo because we can't look at each other. I talked with several foreigners; however I can't talk to foreigners, even Davies, in real life. It was exciting. Very exciting. That sounds good at all, but there are some trouble. Our computer environment is not still enough. If we all had had our own computer and internet had been available in full time, our activety would have been more successful. J building is always crowded and telephone buill is very high in Japan. I don't want connect internet before 23:00. We needed more time available because we had to learn a lot of things to do something in Moo. It is very challenging to learn the ways of speaking, mailing, and making a part of the world. Surely, there are some obstacle, but I'm sure that Moo is one of interesting comunication tools which enable us to study English. I will continue to live in Moo.

Figure 6.5: A Japanese learner's (20) evaluation of the GrassRoots project

Recommendations

Setting up a successful on-line language learning experience requires careful forward planning. Our experiences emphasise that no matter how enthusiastic both learners and teachers are about a project, several factors must be taken into account (Figure 6.6).

Factor	Result	GrassRoots experience
Time zones	Learners should be able to communicate easily in real time. Partners in similar time zones should be grouped together.	Initial groupings included learners from Australia and Sweden. The time difference meant that, eventually, groups had to be changed; Swedes and Ukrainians worked together, while Japanese and Australians collaborated (the Koreans could not be persuaded to MOO by their teacher).
Pedagogy	Teachers must understand the purpose of the project. In order to facilitate this, and to share experiences, it is necessary to have regular (weekly) online meetings with all teachers, even if this requires the adminstrator to organise different meeting for teachers in different time zones - MOO logs can be exchanged to keep different group members appraised of their colleagues' discussion.	Initially, the administrator did not organise official meetings for the GrassRoots project. It soon became apparent that teachers did not understand the purpose of the project (several of them sent messages asking what this was), and regular meetings were implemented as a result, although it was difficult for all teachers to meet at the same time.
Motivation	Learners must be encouraged to communicate with their partners, or motivation will decrease rapidly. It is important for teachers to monitor student: student communication and to encourage it, if it appears to have broken down.	Although some learners **did** communicate with their partners, many did not. Learners who sent messages and received no reply were disappointed and many lost motivation for the project. Since MOO, unlike text chat applications, supports both synchronous and asynchronous methods of communication, learners' failure to use the latter means of contacting peer group members suggests that it is necessary to stress that **all** types (not just synchronous) of exchange of information within the VLE is communication and should be used.
Activities	Learners should be acquainted with MOO and relatively confident about 'speaking' with other MOO users before participating in a project. 'Warm-up' activities should provide the stimulus for more substantial learning activities.	Those students who participated in the warm-up activities (Australian and Swedish) proved to be the most enthusiastic about the project as a whole. This would appear to support the hypothesis about the importance of acquainting learners with MOO before involving them in a learning experience.
Time	Ensure that learning activities are not too ambitious for the time available. In practice, this means that around 6-9 months should be devoted to learners participating in the online activity, while up to another 3 months should be reserved for setting up the activity, clarifying its purpose, communicating with partner teachers, etc.	Several 'warm-up' activities were devised. These were to be completed before moving on to the 'main event'. Unfortunately, there was insufficient time for all activities to be completed and learners moved straight to the main event without participating in the warm-up activities.

Table 6.6: Recommendations for MOO activities

Conclusion

While classroom discourse is largely artificial, even in the most communicative of approaches, MOO offers learners an opportunity to participate in authentic, real time discourse and collaboration with native and non-native speakers of the target language via an accessible technology which allows them to record everything that happens in the VLE for later reading and reflection. This is not to say that the linguistic and communication skills acquired in class are irrelevant or of little use in an on-line situation, quite the contrary; even common initial topics like talking about the weather acquire a high degree of communicative authenticity once participants in a discourse are distributed all over the globe.

From SofiS to stewey, Thursday, 18th November
```
Hello
Hi stewey!
I am fine. Here in sweden we have snow now!!! I just LOVE snow!!!!!!
```

Figure 6.7: MOOmail from a Swedish learner (16) to a Ukrainian learner (19)

Mastering interaction and real time communication in the target language is extremely motivating as is socialising with users from other cultures and linguistic backgrounds. Becoming integrated into L2-mediated communities is possibly one of the most engaging ways of enhancing language learning, since the learner now has a real purpose for learning L2.

Finally, for any who doubt the motivating factors offered to language learners by MOO, one of the most encouraging, and telling, evaluations of the GrassRoots Project came from a 16 year-old Australian student with learning difficulties: *'It was the best and I had the best time here.'*

Bibliography

Shield L and M J Weininger, 'Collaboration in a Virtual World – groupwork and the distance language learner' In Debski R & Levy M (eds.), *WorldCALL: Global Perspectives on Computer Assisted Language Learning* Amsterdam: Swets & Zeitlinger, 99–116. (1999)

Shneiderman B, 'Relate-Create-Donate: A teaching/learning philosophy for the cyber-generation' *Computers & Education,* Vol 31(1): 25–39. (1998) On-line: <ftp://ftp.cs.umd.edu/pub/hcil/Reports-Abstracts-Bibliography/97-17html/97-17.html>

PROJECT WEBSITES

Bamburgh Project, <http://halley.yadata.com.br/schMOOze/MA>

GrassRoots Project, <http://halley.yadata.com.br/schMOOze/GR> Web-based MOO tutorial

Sheld, L and M J Weininger with M Kötter (1999) *Introduction to MOO*, On-line: www.well.ac.uk/wellclass/moo/moo.htm

MOOs

GrassRoots MOO, telnet health.acor.org:8888, Web Interface, <http://health.acor.org/grassroots/java/>, *Homepage*, www.enabling.org/grassroots/

SchMOOze University MOO, telnet schmooze.hunter.cuny.edu:8888, *Web Interface*, <http://schmooze.hunter.cuny.edu> *Homepage*, <http://schmooze.hunter.cuny.edu:8888>

Glossary

IRC — Internet Relay Chat. A text chat system using channels. Only chat is available. There is no other text-based environment with which users may interact.

MOO — Multi User Domain (or Dungeon) Object Oriented. A MOO is a text-based environment or 'world of words'. Users may interact with each other synchronously or asynchronously, as well as with the environment itself.

URL — Universal Resource Locator. The 'address' for a Web page or ftp resource.

VLE — Virtual Learning Environment. A VLE and provides learners with on-line learning opportunities which involve interaction with any or all of the following: software, other learners, teachers/tutors.

Chapter 7

Developing reading skills using the Internet: A school-based study

Helen M. Wright

Background to study

This study developed from a desire to explore the integration of the Internet into programmes of study for secondary school pupils in Years 9–13. Since I have had increasing access to the Internet at school, I have been interested in how best to use it with pupils, partly to evaluate if it was worth using, partly to explore if we were using it to its best advantage. Promoted initially as a source of ready authentic material, the Internet soon proved only marginally more useful in this regard than old-fashioned newspapers –cheaper and more immediate, yes, but with concomitant technical and access problems. I was prompted to ask '*why the Internet?*', and in a search for an answer, I began to compare how I used the Internet for my personal use with how I was asking my pupils to use it. I discovered that I was fascinated by the Internet because of its unpredictability – '*where would this link take me? what is out there for me to find?*' – and by the actions (effectively, research skills) I had to engage in to find what I was looking for. In doing all of this, of course, I was reading the text on the screen, making decisions about which links to follow based on my understanding of what they had to offer. When I reached pages that might be blind alleys, I was learning to make quicker and quicker decisions about whether to click on the Back button on my browser or whether to wait and read on. These skills – gist reading, skim-reading, guessing at the meaning of words from their context, speed reading – were all skills that I was keen for my pupils to develop for exam success as well as for authentic task practice, and I also wanted to see if it was possible to use this medium to encourage pupils to want to read more, drawing on their curiosity. It was out of this that I gradually began to develop my practice and understanding, introducing Internet search activities into class work within the context of a growing awareness about reading skills; this led to a formal study to bring together these strands in September 1999.

The study

The study involved an initial cohort of 21 Year 12 and 13 pupils from four different teaching groups studying A Level French or German, seventeen of whom completed the study over a term and a half. All classes were taught by the same teacher. While this study was based in the sixth form, it was not intended to be exclusive of other year groups, and classes in Years 9 to 11 during this period were also involved in Internet reading skills work. The sixth form classes, however, differed in that they had a regular weekly lesson in the computer room which was devoted to developing reading skills using the Internet, and two evaluation periods, one after 2–3 weeks of such classes, and one after a term. The aim of the study was to discover if individuals showed any discernible improvement in their reading skills over this time, so although the pupils came from different base points, this did not matter – what mattered was the value that this approach added to their reading skills.

The idea of reading skills was not alien to any of the pupils (most of them had encountered the concept of sub-skills such as gist-reading and skimming in study-skills lessons), and prior to the course I used a target language newspaper article in class to start a discussion on what reading might involve. It is important to recognise that this exploration of how the Internet might help improve reading was not intended to be done in isolation from, or at the expense of, other reading activities – the driving purpose behind the study (and the earlier theorising and experimenting with practice) was to investigate the integration of the Internet into programmes of study. The pupils did not read German or French solely on the Internet during the period of the study, although a significant proportion of their class reading was on-line. It was the intention of the evaluations, however, to draw out how using the Internet might help their general reading skill development.

With this in mind, a programme was devised whereby each week these pupils were set tasks that enabled them to practise reading using the Internet. The exercises were varied and often multi-skill (e.g. find out about what has been going on in France/Germany this week and prepare notes for an oral presentation; choose an article, read it and describe it in a letter to a friend), but they each had one thing in common – they relied on the pupils having to search for and find information using the Internet. The first evaluation sheet, after 2–3 weeks, asked each pupil to complete three tasks –to choose three articles on the Internet, read them quickly and think about how much they had understood, before answering the following questions:

1. Which reading skills do you think you have practised in this exercise?
2. How important do you feel reading is to your understanding of French/German?
3. How do you think you can improve your reading skills?

Questions 1 and 2 were intended to promote further discussion of the sorts of skills that readers used, with a growing self-awareness of their own skills. Question 3 encouraged them to think about improvement. Their written comments formed the basis of an individual feedback session with the teacher, where the focus was on how the pupils could improve their reading skills based on what they were doing and learning to do in class. The weekly tasks continued, and after a term, the pupils were given a second evaluation sheet in the same format, with three tasks (exactly as in the first evaluation) intended to focus the pupils on thinking about their reading skills. The questions were slightly different this time:

1 Which reading skills do you think you have practised in these exercises?

2 How does your awareness of reading skills now compare to the first time you did these exercises?

3 Have you improved your reading in any way since the beginning of term? how?

4 How do you think you can improve your reading skills?

Questions 1 and 4 were designed to allow some form of comparison with the first evaluation; questions 2 and 3 (which in practice were treated as nigh identical and answered accordingly), were intended to give some insight into how useful and worthwhile the Internet was as a resource in helping the development of these pupils' reading skills by asking them to identify what it was that they had done to improve their reading.

Evaluation and results of the study

There were three main findings: firstly, all of the pupils who participated in this study were sure that their reading skills had improved, some of them emphatically. All of them appreciated the structured weekly reading session on the Internet. In the feedback sessions there was a real sense of achievement, which was encouraging. It was useful in this respect, and in the absence of a control group (which would have been ethically unsound, given that teacher-researchers in school have a responsibility to ensure equality of opportunity, and in this case, previous informal classroom experiments had suggested that using the Internet might well help develop reading skills), to have a range of pupils of different abilities and different year groups – all of the Year 13 pupils also felt that they had made significant progress. It was difficult to find an objective means of judging progress that isolated the effect of using the Internet on reading skills (many aspects of the pupils' learning and teaching could have contributed to their higher exam results in December) – I felt, however, that isolation was counterproductive to mixed-skills learning, and I felt it important to trust in my relationship with the pupils in establishing whether they were accurately reporting their progress – a valid qualitative means of evaluation. As the study progressed, the importance of the interconnectedness of learning became clearer – on reflection, I could also have looked more closely in the study at how it impacted on the pupils' general learning skills.

Secondly, there was an increased awareness of reading skills, evident in the greater degree of clarity about reading skills and their own reading profiles that the pupils exhibited in the second feedback session. A broad range of reading and learning to read skills received mention in the response to Question 3 in the second evaluation: reading more/regularly (8), developing confidence through practice (4), skimming/picking out key words (4), reading for gist/understanding the theme (4), increasing knowledge of vocabulary (4), learning to guess from context (3), increasing knowledge of cultural context (2), using the dictionary (2), increasing knowledge of grammar (1). This awareness of skills had an observable spin-off in class reading work and exam practice: in class discussions during and after the period of study, explicit links made briefly by the teacher between skills such as skimming and quick reading, practised or developed while using the Internet, and the skills needed to tackle exam questions quickly or read a newspaper, were readily accepted and agreed with by the pupils.

Thirdly, there was a significant increase (from two mentions in the first evaluation to eleven in the second) in the number of participants who felt that to improve their reading skills, they needed to read more widely. This was encouraging because it suggested that the pupils regarded reading as a universal activity and not one limited to the Internet and therefore non-transferable. It might also be hypothesised that the experience of the pupils in exploring the Internet had led them to appreciate the variety of texts and language around, and/or that they may have recognised that if they kept to similar sites, the language they encountered remained similar, which in turn may have led them to appreciate the importance of variety. In any case, this outcome was a desirable one.

Apart from this encouraging result, the study did not show significant changes in responses to either of the direct comparison questions. When asked how they felt they could improve their reading, the pupils posited '*reading more*' (first evaluation: 19; second: 13 – perhaps the fewer numbers of pupils in the second indicated that some felt they were now reading more) and '*expanding vocabulary*' (6; 6). It was unsurprising to find that they did not come up with new and creative ways of improving – what they did suggest was perfectly sound! Their answers to the question of which skills they were practising in the reading tasks were equally unsurprising, as on both evaluation occasions, the tasks largely involved gist reading, skim reading and reading quickly, which most pupils mentioned. This question could be used, however, to distinguish between types of reader, from the less sophisticated reader who described it as '*general reading*' to the more sophisticated reader who mentioned '*gist reading, skim reading, reading quickly, guessing from context, summarising and understanding grammar*'. This data was useful for the teacher in identifying pupil needs for future attention; the individual profiles of the pupils that emerged from their responses to each evaluation enabled the teacher to track their progress in a more precise way than would have been possible without the study.

Conclusion and comments

On balance, then, this study was a success: it showed that using the Internet to develop reading skills was worthwhile and motivating. The evaluation intrinsic to the study was also useful in providing teacher and pupils with information about the pupils' reading skills and in emphasising the importance of these skills. In fact, the value of the evaluations was such that they demonstrate clearly the value to practising teachers of engaging in this type of classroom-based research. I am already using similar search and find Internet activities with all classes (even beginners), with observable positive effects in reading skills development and motivation, and I recommend them.

Chapter 8

Videoconferencing case studies

Philip Dobison and Garry Hudson

Case Study 1: Cranford Community College

Philip Dobison

Background

Cranford Community College has been equipping itself with a whole raft of ICT facilities for some time, so that it can best prepare its students for the new millennium. By the time the college successfully achieved Language College Status in September 1997, ICT use was a familiar part of a number of curriculum areas. The new status meant that the level and range of facilities could be extended. This was heralded most clearly by the arrival of the interactive whiteboard and videoconferencing facilities. Since this time, the College has been involved in three different types of use of videoconferencing.

Cranford serves a very diverse community in terms of ethnic background, culture and linguistic heritage. Our Language College bid reflected this diversity and we are now able to offer eleven languages; French, German, Spanish, Italian, Russian, Japanese, Mandarin Chinese, Panjabi, Hindi, Urdu and Gujerati. The student body, however, has a range of languages that goes well beyond this, numbering 40-plus in total. Our plans therefore were to create an inclusive linguistic environment, in which all students would have access to a native speaker of their home language and of their second or third language. We also aim to increase the awareness of our student body of their role over the next century as citizens of a world which is ever-shrinking, ever more exciting, yet ever more challenging.

For the European languages that we teach, we are able to bring in foreign language assistants (FLAs) from these countries or have teachers who are also native speakers. The same is true for the Community Languages we teach. The first real challenges came from the Arabic speaking community. We do not have an Arabic speaker within the staff, but we know a man who does, and so we began to work closely with the British Airways Dubai office to enable us to videoconference with native Arabic speakers. This project was featured on BBC Breakfast Time, during which the BBC's broadcast link between the school and Television Centre broke down, while our link remained intact.

The College has been using *A level 2000*[1] since September 1998 to augment its language teaching within the college. This package involves students' participating in an individual videoconference every week. The scheme revolves around work on CD-ROMs that students complete and e-mail to the tutor, who then assesses and manages the student's learning programme.

The third type of conference is based around international communication to increase understanding of the world and its young people. A good example of this emanates from our membership of I*EARN (International Education and Resource Network). We were approached by Washington High School, in Wisconsin, USA, who were planning a visit for some of its students to Europe. For many this would be the first trip away from their local state, let alone abroad. The teachers wished their students to have first-hand knowledge of what living in the UK was like, so that they might feel more at ease on their journey.

Preparation for conferences

All systems have time lags between the person speaking and being received at the other end. Consequently, it is important that there is clear direction about who is to speak and when. Our prerequisite for any conference is that we have a dry run for the teachers beforehand; firstly, to ensure the systems being used are compatible; secondly, to ensure they work; thirdly, to talk through the conference and draw up a game plan of what is being covered. A game plan is vital to facilitate the progress of the conference and to avoid pregnant pauses or over-talking. The game plan needs to consider such protocols as who speaks first, who manages the conference, how people are addressed, and should include a list of participants (if a large conference), and consider how long the conference is going to be, and so on. It does, however, need to be flexible as we cannot always foresee how the discussions will develop. For whole-group conferences, we use a roving microphone so that we can ensure our participants don't over-talk and this is a clear signal to the other end that our participant is ready to speak. The same is not an issue for conferences involving individuals.

What if it goes wrong?

The answer is – it does – and it will – and usually when the technician is not around. With the regular weekly videoconferences, we train the students in how to set up the conference on the videoconference PC. We also train anyone who is going to be involved in conferencing in how to set up the conference and offer layman's advice on how to troubleshoot. This includes use of the address book/contact list, so that re-dialling is not an issue, nor is incorrect dialling. We always have a separate telephone line and contact available to speak to the other end, should things go wrong.

What our students and tutors think of it

Students are usually apprehensive before their first conferences, and quite understandably so. There is something about the immediacy of the live link-up that means that students have to respond. Students report that their nervousness and anxiety are soon replaced by a feeling of ease. Their motivation to speak remains high. As one student said:

> *It's OK speaking with Martin (the German FLA), because there's less pressure on me to speak, but when I videoconference, I feel a lot more need to speak back quickly and this has made me much more confident and I have to think of what to say much more quickly.*

A review of our short experience has shown that the speaking capabilities of students involved in the weekly videoconferences has risen noticeably, as has their confidence. The students who were involved in the conference with Washington High School felt really excited by the whole experience. It was a very open-ended discussion of youth culture and it was amazing for me as an observer, to see how global youth culture has become. Our students made real friends and are now regularly receiving e-mail contacts from the American students. It has broadened the horizons of both sets of students.

> *I thought that the videoconference was a very good idea to get students around the world to talk to each other and learn about each other's lifestyle. In addition to this we learn what they study and participate in at school. The best thing about it is that you can see whom you are talking to, what you look like, your face expressions and anything silly that you do to people so far away in another country. It was a very amusing experience as Deepi and myself entertained the students a lot and we found out a lot about their lifestyle, habits and interests.* Kanwardeep Dhanjal (Year 13)

Tutors and teachers involved in the videoconferences find them challenging at the beginning – it is new technology, and it needs the tutor to be confident in its use. After the dry run, most teachers feel better about its use and not put off by a lack of knowledge and familiarity.

One teacher explained:

> *The idea of being able to speak to someone across the world, and to see them at the same time is so amazing and exciting. I can hardly believe it is possible. The immediacy of the medium and the impact it has on students who take part is truly huge. A word from a student overseas is worth a thousand of the words I can say. It is so important to hear things from the horse's mouth.*

The future

With the development of faster communications, the future holds exciting prospects for improved vision and audibility. Cranford is planning to extend the use of videoconferencing from September 2000 through its own intranet – conferencing more within the school with FLAs, following the success of the individual conferences with Video 2000. The motivation and immediacy of the conference are spurring students on to greater things, and we are planning to begin action research on the use of ICT and videoconferencing in raising language competencies. We plan to integrate the use of conferencing into our numerous international projects, so that all curriculum areas can contribute to increasing the global awareness of our students.

We continue to seek out international links to enable students to access native speakers, and are looking to expand our range of languages through a mutually beneficial interchange of teaching (Norwegian head teachers were very interested in sharing Norwegian and English lessons in this way). Our Community plan will involve our family of primary schools and secondary schools in conferencing so that we can avoid the travel time and give valuable language input, both on a whole-class and individual basis.

At present, we are just beginning to scratch the surface and are feeling our way through this exciting development. However, one of the inevitable challenges we will face is the structure of the traditional school day, when conferences with Japan and China become commonplace.

Case Study 2: Bishop's Stortford College

Garry Hudson

At Bishop's Stortford College our principal experience of using videoconferencing has been through ParlEuNet, a collaborative project involving schools throughout Europe working on activities based on young people and the European Parliament. At any given time the following scenarios have occurred:

- a conference involving two schools;
- a conference with three schools;
- a conference with three schools including the presence of a Member of the European Parliament.

When students understand how the medium works and prepare each session thoroughly, there is no doubt that videoconferencing can be a great motivating force in enabling groups to speak each other's language and get to know each other's culture better. Our experience shows that videoconferences become much more effective and productive as learners get used to them; they become more confident as foreign language speakers, they will think more about how they appear to others and how to elicit information more effectively from their partners. Our early exchanges, it must be said, were characterised by their novelty value rather than any intrinsic linguistic or cultural value – pupils were eager to become TV personalities in much the same way as football supporters who suddenly become aware that they are on live television and want to be noticed. However, after an early de-briefing, this was addressed and subsequent exchanges became noticeably more positive.

One of our most successful conferences was with the Adolphe Max Athénée in Brussels. The aim was to learn about each other's culture using each other's language. The preparation began two weeks prior to the conference: each group had to choose ten objects which for them represented their culture and they were presented to the other group in pairs. Needless to say, fish and chips, football, Buckingham Palace, etc ranked high on the British list, while *moules frites*, chocolate and Astérix etc were top of the Belgian list. Thorough practice of the appropriate language and structures took place prior to the conference; students were ingenious about finding or creating suitable representations of the items. Football created the most discussion – should they show a Manchester United or Liverpool scarf – and '*how do you say life-long supporter, sir?*' The conference itself began with friendly waves to the students in Brussels whom they knew quite well by this stage, having had several preliminary sessions earlier in the term. English students spoke French and the Belgian students had prepared their exposés in English – it was significant that the teachers in attendance were equally complimentary about the quality of language of their counterparts' students both during the exchange and also during the on-line discussion among teachers after the pupil conference.

The follow-up to this conference, which took place in the classroom, produced more than one could have anticipated. In class much discussion was generated – in the FL of course – about how things went, but what was even more rewarding for the teachers was the fact that students were now contacting each other independently by e-mail. Four pupils had even discussed the real possibility of doing an exchange during the holidays.

In addition to the linguistic and cultural benefit derived from these experiences, the students were encouraged to think critically about the medium of videoconferencing in general. As a result of these discussions between teachers and students, a number of conclusions were drawn which, it was felt, would enhance the benefits of this form of learning and communication:

1. One must understand how the equipment works.
2. The speaker must be relaxed, appreciate that the medium is slow and act accordingly.
3. One must be realistic about the medium: it can do more than any other educational medium, but also much less if not carefully stage-managed.
4. If there is a chairperson, one must be aware of his/her function to manage the session – for example , he or she must be conscious of the duration and fair distribution of speeches.
5. One should look just below the camera and speak clearly and slowly and continuously – often a break in the middle of a sentence is mistaken for the end of a contribution.
6. One should avoid adopting a formal and dry manner in front of the camera – students find that off-putting.
7. One should not make abrupt movements, because it causes the image to blur.
8. The presenter must make the students participate through questions and answers or interactive group activities.
9. Questions should, where possible, be addressed to a specific participant and should also be repeated by the presenter of the other group.
10. Clear rules about allowing others to finish and asking permission to speak and the duration of contributions should be established at the outset.
11. It is necessary to evaluate the atmosphere in the group – this comes with experience and will help to avoid unnecessary silences or embarrassed looks from the participants. For this reason I would recommend that the chairperson be able to move the camera (which is easily manoeuvrable) and be ready to bring in another contributor.
12. Finally, the need for careful preparation and follow-up are indispensable to the success of a conference.

Our experience shows that videoconferencing can be most effective when linked to work using the target language in the classroom and also to a general discussion (in English or in the foreign language) about the relative merits of the experience. In conclusion, I would add that we are still learning to handle this exciting medium and as technology advances and the quality of sound and picture improves, I am sure that videoconferencing will bring language learners of different cultures closer together and enable them to increase their competence in learning foreign languages.

Unfortunately, we were unable to record the conferences which we held with our foreign partner schools and I find it difficult to be precise about the impact on our students' language skills. What I am convinced about, however, is the increase in motivation which has generated the sort of response which I had not anticipated: namely the desire on the part of the students (and the teachers too!) to continue talking, e-mailing and to consider setting up individual and class exchanges. The whole project has taught pupils about each other's culture, the importance of moving away from stereotypical views and how to break down cultural barriers through communication – bilingual or monolingual – '*ça a vraiment créé des liens*'! We have also been able to discuss, in follow-up lessons, the sort of language needed to be able to talk about technology – which the students see as very relevant to today's world. We hope to improve the quality of sound and image (our system is four years old!) by more modern systems, which we hope to set in place during the next academic year. If we are able to use the college IT network for videoconferencing, most of the language teachers will be able to participate from their own classroom and this, I am sure, will help us to maximise the potential of this medium of communication and foreign language teaching.

Notes

1 More information available on www.vektor.com

PART THREE

Initial teacher training

In this final part there is a chapter in which Fairtlough considers a training programme which he designed as an introduction to the use of ICT in language learning for a group of trainee teachers. Whilst not an action research study in itself, it nevertheless contributes to this volume both in topic and in spirit. The author reflects upon the ongoing changes in teaching and learning brought about through new technologies. He also considers the longer term implications for tomorrow's teachers. Will the languages teachers of the future be imbued with a knowledge of ICT before they reach the training college? Already, he detects signs of heightened awareness of the medium stemming from their personal use of applications such as e-mail, Internet and word processing. Experience of having used ICT in their own language learning is still uncommon, but this too may change rapidly.

It is not just teaching and learning that are changing but teachers also. *'I became a languages teacher because I wanted to develop virtual learning'* is not a quote from one of Fairtlough's students but it is apparent from this chapter that there is considerable engagement by student teachers with the application of ICT to language learning.

Chapter 9

Training student teachers to use ICT for MFL

Harry Fairtlough

In September 1998 I was asked to provide a course of twelve sessions of two hours each to train student teachers at Westminster College, Oxford, to use ICT for teaching MFL. My own background is that of a practising freelance secondary teacher of Spanish and French with a strong interest and some expertise in ICT. The requirements of the Teacher Training Agency, detailing the ICT competence levels required of newly qualifying teachers, had just been published and in my course plan I attempted to take these on board while setting as my main priority the need to give the trainees the confidence actually to use (and to demand to use) ICT in their teaching practice. The course would be delivered in a computer room with 30 machines (there were 27 students) for ten weeks with two sessions subsequent to the trainees' main period with their schools. The course would be definitely competence-based, aiming to improve the trainees' own computer skills at the same time as indicating ways to incorporate ICT into their teaching.

Course outline

Session 1	Introduction
Session 2	Activities using WORD
Session 3	Further Activities using WORD and PAINT
Session 4	Activity using ACCESS
Session 5	Activity using EXCEL
Session 6	Introduction to the Internet as a teaching/learning tool
Session 7	KS3 and KS4 Activities using the Internet
Session 8	KS5 Activities using the Internet
Session 9	Dedicated Language Learning Software
	Assessment of ICT in the NC
	Do's and Don't's in the Computer Room
	Bibliography

Session 10 Trainee assessment procedures
Establishment of portfolio
Polishing up two activities to be delivered in schools

(two months later)

Session 11 Follow up of work in schools
Evaluation of course

Session 12 Activity using POWERPOINT

The introductory session tried to put ICT into the context of secondary schools at that time and to establish an audit of the trainees' current ICT competence through self-evaluation. This latter revealed some familiarity with word processing, but little else. I was surprised, until I realised that this cohort would have missed out on much of what was currently being done in schools. One explanation may be that, although there have been many interesting ICT developments in schools over the past decade, language teachers and their students may not have been involved as schools gave priority to traditional ICT subjects like maths, science, technology and business. The audit was carried out with tick boxes on two sheets of A4 with questions of the type *'Can you create a database/If so, can you sort and search? What database software have you used?'* Excessive jargon and technical terms were avoided but there was enough to differentiate between those who really could and those who couldn't. And anyway, it was stressed that an honest audit would, in fact, make the course far more beneficial for all. From one year to another there was a noticeable increase in the number of trainees with e-mail/Internet experience. With the overall raising of trainees' competency, this type of audit needs to be reviewed for each new cohort: for example, for the following September, I would definitely include questions on web page creation and use of sound files.

This session ended with discussion of the question *'Why use ICT to teach/learn languages?'* As many of the trainees had never used ICT for MFL, the responses were minimal; for example *'It's fun!, Surf the Net'*. However, there was enough curiosity to want to find better answers. Students were given the task of practising their word processing skills before the next session, which opened with an activity designed to start them thinking about the role of ICT in language learning.

This activity attempted from the start to distinguish the main aim (learning elements of the target language) from the tool (ICT). The setting of a simple activity also enabled even the weakest trainees (from an ICT perspective) to produce worthwhile work. The opportunity was also taken to establish some points of good practice such as the inclusion of extension work (in this case, adding clipart) and the need to have names on work. Once the resulting worksheets were printed out, each trainee carried out the activity of another and had to provide constructive criticism. This was very effective in highlighting the requirements of worksheets (clarity of task and outcome, visual attraction and compatibility with pupils' prior learning both in ICT and MFL).

This approach was adopted for the following six sessions when similar worksheets at various levels were prepared and tested, using a drawing program, a database, a spreadsheet and the Internet. For each of these applications some very brief training was included, but the onus was clearly on the trainee to practise the relevant package before the next session. In fact, once the trainees had appreciated the value of ICT for their teaching, their own competence was never really a problem. I tried to make sure that at least one trainee within the group was able to carry out the basic operations required (e.g. copying text and graphics from the Web into a word processor document) and thereby be a team leader in assisting the others. By the time that activities based on the Web were being prepared for sixth formers, the quality of the worksheets was what could be expected from postgraduate students. (See Session Plan 3 in Figure 9.1 and Session Plan 6 in Figure 9.2.)

SESSION 3

In this session each trainee will devise a language learning activity using ICT and then the activity devised will be carried out by another intern who will then comment on the activity. This activity can be done in the language of your choice.

SCENARIO

Year 9 have now been studying a foreign language for two and half years. They are repeating in greater depth some of the topics covered in Year 7. The students can use WORD competently and are able to do their own drawings in PAINT and import them into a WORD document as well as using the CLIPART file.

The activity will be based on the topic:

My home

and should incorporate:

- **the rooms in the house**
- **what is in the rooms**
- **what the student (and the family) does in the rooms**

Task 1 (Devising the activity)

- Word process a work sheet giving instructions for the activity to be carried out by Year 9.

Task 2 (Carrying out and commenting on the activity)

- Follow the instructions and complete the activity devised by another intern.
- Below your completed work, briefly comment on:
  - The merits of the activity for learning the target language
  - Any problems encountered in carrying out the activity

Figure 9.1: Session Plan 3

SESSION 6

Using the Internet to enhance teaching and learning

Exporting text and materials:
- Print outs
- Text to WORD
- Save picture as file
- Pictures to WORD via Print Screen and PAINT
- Save as HTML file
- Save as plain text
- Save sound and animation files

Further reading

Usborne – 101 things to do on the Internet
CILT – The Web by Terry Atkinson
Target 2000 on www.nelson.co.uk

Session activity

Objective
To devise two learning activities (one for KS3 and one for KS4) each based on one or more websites. Possible topics:

- Plan a journey
- Compare lives of celebrities
- Cook book
- Make a brochure of a town
- Manual for a leisure time pursuit
- Make a poster on a social issue

Your tasks (in WORD):

1. *Description of activity* (for teacher)
   - Objectives
   - Outcomes (with extensions)
   - Level
   - Topic/structures/websites (URL)
   - Prior learning ICT/TL
   - Time required for basic activity
   - On-line/Off-line/Print out follow up

2. *Worksheet* (for students) including ICT/MFL assessment arrangements (e.g. 2/20 marks for title/name). Inclusion of some graphics might be appropriate. Please print out on 4 separate sheets of A4 and staple together.

Figure 9.2: Session Plan 6

Session 9 was the only really non-practical part of the course. We looked at dedicated language learning software (or rather the lack of it). *Fun with Texts* was mentioned but, realising that many trainees might find this the only resource available in their schools, I stressed the need to prepare their own materials and for all trainees to build up their own portfolio of suitable activities. A bibliography was provided in the form of a short list of websites including BECTA, Linguanet and several university sites. Further brief mention was made of assessment of ICT within the National Curriculum and what language teachers might be expected to do in this respect. The session ended with a lively discussion in which a list of *Do's and Don'ts in the Computer Room* (Figure 9.3) was compiled from trainees' suggestions. The work of a single MFL teacher in a computer room with 30 students can be very rewarding; it can also be very stressful, with target language pressures and unpredictable ICT problems, so strategies to minimize eventual problems are essential.

Do	Don't
Prepare activities very carefully	Use students' mouse and keyboard
Ensure that prior learning has taken place	Spend excessive time with one student
Write instructions very clearly	Try to solve unknown problems at students' computer
Check out hardware/software in advance	Allow one student of a pair to do all the work
Set clear outcome which all can achieve (including saving and printing)	Despair when all goes wrong at once
Prepare extension activity, perhaps open ended	
Have clear idea of assessment for both ICT and TL in advance	
Prioritise requests for help	
Use TL as much as possible	
Have contingency plans	

Figure 9.3: Some do's and don'ts in the Computer Room

The final session started with a detailed explanation of how the trainees would themselves be assessed. The assessment of the trainees' own competence was, in fact, outside my remit and all I was asked to do was to ensure that they completed the final check list of competencies with a note of the relevant evidence. However, I was determined that an assessment of their ability to deliver MFL through ICT should be based on actual delivery to real pupils in a school. The ICT coordinator in the relevant school was involved in the process so as both to ensure that some independent observation of the activity was made and that facilities for the activity were made available in the school. The trainees completed this session by polishing up, with some input from myself, their two selected activities, one of which would be delivered.

There were a number of practical problems involved at the school end: room not available; ICT coordinator unwilling to observe; activities selected not suitable for the classes allocated. However, all trainees did manage to deliver at least one activity, some did more, and to complete the relevant paperwork. This comprised:

- a detailed lesson plan;
- at least three pupil outcomes;
- a report from the ICT coordinator;
- and the trainee's own evaluation of the session.

I had given the trainees my home e-mail address should they have any problems or queries during the course. It was interesting that this offer was only taken up on this one issue of delivery of the activity in school and the subsequent assessment.

On return from the schools we had two final sessions, with feedback from each trainee on their specific experience in schools followed by evaluation of the course in groups. The most general comment from their feedback was that they felt that they were way ahead, in terms of wanting to use ICT and being able to, of most of the colleagues in the schools they had visited. This was a reassuring comment for myself. The final session was devoted to presentation software with a brief introduction, with a presentation from myself about the usage of *verdad, también* and *tampoco* in Spanish. Then all trainees prepared and delivered their own presentations which were voted on in Eurovision song contest style, which provided a suitable conclusion to a course which both teacher and students appeared to have enjoyed.

For the year 1999–2000, I was asked to repeat the course but with fewer hours and fewer trainees. Even with just the twelve months difference, I found the initial ICT skills of this group far more advanced than those of the previous year and it was not difficult to repeat virtually all the elements of the course within the reduced hours. For the future this trend should be accentuated, with trainee teachers arriving with wider ICT skills and also their own language learning experiences through ICT. More time can thereby be devoted to analysing what elements of a given language may best be learned with the assistance of ICT and to evaluating how individual pupils respond to tasks based on ICT. With more resources becoming available on the Web, including worksheets relating to specific textbooks and specific pages of those textbooks, the emphasis may move away from the need for teachers and trainees to develop their own resources towards a competence in evaluating what is already available. However, given the nature of ICT, there will always be new applications for the innovative teacher to learn and apply to their own teaching. Who would have said five years ago that the oral presentation at GCSE could be delivered using presentation software?

Contributors

Jim Anderson is Lecturer in Modern Languages in Education at Goldsmiths' College, University of London. He has a particular interest in bilingualism and is a member of the CILT Advisory Group for Community Languages.

Terry Atkinson is a Senior Lecturer in Education (Modern Languages) at the University of Bristol working mainly in the areas of initial and in-service teacher training.

Larry Davies is an Associate Professor at Future University, Hakodate, Hokkaido, Japan. His current interests lie in the design, implementation, troubleshooting and management of Internet-mediated collaborative learning environments.

Philip Dobison is the Language College Manager at Cranford Community College in West London. He has taught Modern Foreign Languages for twenty years and is responsible for International Curriculum links for the college.

Harry Fairtlough was, at the time of writing a visiting lecturer at Westminster College, Oxford, and a part time secondary teacher of Spanish and French with a specific interest in ICT. Currently, he is working in the area of on-line teaching.

Lesley Hagger-Vaughan is Senior Teacher at Shireland Language College and Principal Examiner for GCSE German at Edexcel.

Sue Hewer is a freelance consultant in ICT and language learning with a special interest in the use of internet telephony to enable distance and isolated learners to develop interactive oral fluency.

Garry Hudson is Head of Modern Languages at Bishop's Stortford College where he teaches French and Japanese. His school has recently been involved in a European project using videoconferencing to communicate with students in other countries.

Heather Rendall works as an independent advisory teacher, specialising in language acquisition and ICT & MFL. Her previous publications include: *Pathfinder 33: Stimulating grammatical awareness* (CILT) and *Effective MFL grammar teaching* (Folens). She also works as a consultant for publishers and produced the ICT activities for the *Mach's Gut* course (Nelson-Thornes).

Lesley Shield is a Lecturer in Language Learning and Technology at the Open University. She works primarily with the use of synchronous computer-mediated communication and distance learning.

Markus Weininger is a Lecturer in German Language and Literature at the Federal University of Santa Catarina in Southern Brazil. He works with ICT for language learning and also lectures on pedagogical uses of the Internet.

David Wilson works in the Equal Opportunities Department at Harton School in South Shields, teaching French and German; he works particularly with pupils with special educational needs.

Helen Wright is Deputy Head at Heathfield School, Ascot. She conducted the research that forms the basis of her chapter in her previous post, as Head of German and teacher of French and German to A Level at St Edward's School, Oxford.